In *Image of the Holy Spirit and the Church* Stephen Hiemstra teaches us about the third person of the Trinity—the Holy Spirit. The Holy Spirit is the most misunderstood person of the Godhead, but also the most essential. Jesus told us he would not leave us orphaned, and he asked his heavenly Father to send the comforter, the Holy Spirit who will teach you and remind you of all the things Jesus spoke. There can be no spirit-filled life without the Holy Spirit. We live in his dispensation until Jesus returns. God's peace, encouragement, guidance, and authority to minister all originate from the Holy Spirit.

Stephen's books are exceptionally written, and each nugget of wisdom is captioned with thought-provoking questions that deepen our understanding of and draw us closer to God. This book is an indispensable addition to his *Image of God* series that will deepen your spiritual walk with the Lord.

Eric Teitelman
House of David Ministries

"A footloose Holy Spirit" and an "Avian image of God" splash vivid word pictures on a canvas depicting the role of the Holy Spirit in the Church. Stephen Hiemstra, in *Image of the Holy Spirit and the Church,* writes of the Holy Spirit's essential role in the Body of Christ in a lively manner that is both scholarly and comprehensible for those who wish to understand more about the third person of the Trinity.

Sharron Giambanco

* *The Image of the Holy Spirit and the Church* helps believers to dive deeper into the Holy Spirit's role in establishing the early church and churches today. Stephen Hiemstra's book covers topics related to the Holy Spirit with a special focus on the Gospels of Luke and John, as part of Hiemstra's Image of God series.

Sarah Hamaker

Author, The Cold War Legacy series

Image of God Series:

Image of God in the Parables

Christian Spirituality Series:

A Christian Guide to Spirituality[1]

Life in TensionCalled Along the Way[2]

Simple Faith

Living in Christ

Image and Illumination

Masquerade Series:[3]

Masquerade

The Detour

Prayerbooks:

Everyday Prayers for Everyday People

Prayers[4]

Prayers of a Life in Tension

---

1 Also available in Spanish and German.
2 Also available in Spanish.
3 Screenplays have been adapted from these books.
4 Also available in Spanish.

IMAGE OF THE HOLY SPIRIT AND THE CHURCH

Forgotten Path in Winter

IMAGE OF THE HOLY SPIRIT AND THE CHURCH

Stephen W. Hiemstra

T2P

T2Pneuma Publishers LLC
Centreville, Virginia

IMAGE OF THE HOLY SPIRIT AND THE CHURCH

T2Pneuma Publishers LLC
P.O. Box 230564, Centreville, Virginia 20120
www.T2Pneuma.com

Names: Hiemstra, Stephen Wayne, author. Title: Image of the Holy Spirit and the Church / by Stephen W. Hiemstra. Series: Image of God Description: Includes bibliographical reference and index. | Centreville, VA: T2Pneuma Publishers LLC, 2023. Identifiers: LCCN: 2023918986 | ISBN: 978-1-942199-86-1 (paperback) | 978-1-942199-46-5 (KDP) | 978-1-942199-77-9 (epub) Subjects: LCSH Holy Spirit. | Christian life. | BISAC RELIGION / Christian Theology / Pneuma-tology Classification: LCC BT121.2 .H54 2023 | DDC 231/.3--dc23

Many thanks to my editors, Sarah Hamaker and Jean Arnold, for their prompt and precise work.

Cover art by C. Hiemstra (2023), The Lighthouse,
Used with Permission.
Cover by SWH

CONTENTS

PREFACE

The earth was without form and void,

and darkness was over the face of the deep.

And the Spirit of God was hovering

over the face of the waters.

(Gen 1:2)

*I*f the Bible is an outreach document written by and for missionaries (Schnabel 2004, 5-6), then the Holy Spirit is the agent of that evangelistic call. *The Image of the Holy Spirit and the Church* examines the Bible's description of the Holy Spirit from before Pentecost and the call of the church in view of current challenges.

My recent book, *Image and Illumination* (2023), asked the question "What does it mean to be created in the image of God?" with a focus on Christian anthropology. Embedded in this question is the metaphysical question: Who is God? The New Testament addresses this question with three pictures of God: The person of Jesus, Jesus' teaching about God the Father in the parables, and the founding of the church on Pentecost by the Holy Spirit. In this book, I focus on the image of the Holy Spirit and the church.

The Postmodern Dilemma

Nietzsche was the son of a Lutheran pastor and knew what it meant to be a Christian. Today we confront sons and daughters of Nietzsche who overlook his insanity, eagerly grasp his will-to-power teaching, and have no clue as to what Christianity is about.

The simultaneous declines of life expectancy, fertility, and standards of living—presumably, preventable problems—parallel a curse for ignoring the Mosaic covenant:

> You shall betroth a wife, but another man shall ravish her. You shall build a house, but you shall not dwell in it. You shall plant a vineyard, but you shall not enjoy its fruit. (Deut 28:30)

Delbert Hillers (1964, 78-79) characterizes these afflictions as futility curses. Today's new age religion might call these bad karma, but the Bible suggests that luck has nothing to do with it—they result from turning your back on the living God.

Loving the wrong things so much that you fail to attend to the natural priorities in life—health, family and work—suggests a spiritual problem at the heart of these ostensibly secular issues.

In the midst of cultural meltdown and churchly amnesia, ecclesiology—study of the church—remains untiled soil.

Old Testament Images

While the church as we know it is a product of the New Testament, antecedents of the church can be found in the image and work of the Holy Spirit in the Old Testament.

The avian image of God's spirit found in Genesis 1:2 contrasts primordial chaos with a God who brings order. The Holy Spirit embodies God's agency in the world and brings order through his words in creation, covenants to his people, and promises to his elect.

The Holy Spirit in Luke-Acts

The Holy Spirit is footloose in the Book of Acts as named and unnamed disciples carry the Gospel to Jerusalem, Judea, Samaria, and the ends of the earth (Acts 1:8). At the council of Jerusalem, in spite of much opposition, the Gospel is provisionally opened to Gentiles (Acts 15:19-20). The Gospel reached the farthermost parts of the Roman Empire and beyond within a single generation. The purpose of the spirit in evangelism is to identify those called to be the church, often called "The Way" in the Book of Acts (e.g. 19:9, 19:23, 24:14, 24:22).

The Church in Paul's Writing

The Apostle Paul's work as an evangelist is mixed with the heart of a pastor in his letters to the churches. Listen to Paul in his letter to the church at Corinth:

> To those sanctified in Christ Jesus, called to be saints together with all those who in every place call upon the name of our Lord Jesus Christ, both their Lord and ours. (1 Cor 1:2)

The phrase—called to be saints together—suggests both that our purpose in being called is to become more holy and that this process can only be attained jointly with others called by God. Paul's favorite description of the church, which is used here, is the "called out ones." Spiritual formation is an important role of the church.

The Spirit in John-Revelation

The agency of the Holy Spirit works in the church to identify and form Christians. Part of this identity is vision-casting, as we see in John's writing. John's writing has at least three distinctives with regard to the Holy Spirit: A high view of scripture, spirit-driven accounts of pastoral care, and images of spirit-inspired worship. Much like heaven and earth are formed together, hearts and minds must be formed together, if the faithful are to believe.

Christian Spirituality

The unity of heart and mind poses a special challenge in today's world where heart and mind are frequently treated as separate with one or the other being emphasized. Neglect of the heart leads to a stale, distant faith while neglect of the mind leads to a superficial faith with little application to daily challenges. The image of a Triune God—Father, Son, and Holy Spirit—reminds us that heart and mind are best taken together.

Image of the Holy Spirit and the Church is the second book in my Image of God series. The first book, *Image of God in the Parables*, studies the image of God the Father found in Jesus' parables. This book focuses on the role of the Holy Spirit. This book is written in a devotional format with a reflection, prayers, and questions for study.

Soli Deo Gloria

∞

Spirit of God,

All praise and honor, power and dominion, truth and justice are yours because you sustain and provision all living things, live within us, and grant us all manner of spiritual gifts. Be ever near.

Forgive our lack of spiritual knowledge, unwillingness to practice forgiveness, and unbecoming, haughty nature. Father of all holiness, create in us clean hearts.

Thank you for teaching us the spiritual gifts of "Love, joy, peace, patience, kindness, goodness, faithfulness, gentleness, and self control." (Gal 5:22-23) May we ever share these gifts with everyone we meet.

Grant us discerning hearts and minds that we might love the things that you love and hate the things that you hate.

In Jesus' precious name, Amen.

∞

Questions
1. What three images of God do we find in the New Testament?
2. What is a son and daughter of Nietzsche?
3. What is the first mention of the Holy Spirit in scripture?
4. What are the two primary objectives of the Holy Spirit in the New Testament?

INTRODUCTION

Synopsis

The introduction provides a summary of the book. It starts with a problem statement for the postmodern church that focuses on the battleground of the human heart darkened by sin, and proceeds to cite evidence from the Old Testament of the Holy Spirit's influence. The remaining sections outline the Holy Spirit's influence in the writings of Luke, Paul, and John.

The Postmodern Dilemma

For although they knew God, they did not honor him as God
or give thanks to him, but they became futile in their thinking,
and their foolish hearts were darkened.

(Rom 1:21)

*T*he battleground of the church is the human heart.

Just before God sent the flood to wipe out all of humanity, except for Noah and his family, we read:

> The LORD saw that the wickedness of man was great in the earth, and that every intention of the thoughts of his heart was only evil continually. And the LORD regretted that he had made man on the earth, and it grieved him to his heart. (Gen 6:5–6)

Notice the phrases, "every intention of the thoughts of his heart," and "grieved him [God] to his heart."

The word *heart* in the Hebrew is *lev* (BDB 4761), which means either "The inner man in contrast with outer" or "The inner man, indef., soul, comprehending mind, affections and will." The Greek translation in the Septuagint is *cardia* (BDAG 3926) that means either "Heart as seat of physical, spiritual and mental life" or "Interior, center, heart." The biblical heart is according closer to the term *soul* and clearly involves both mind and body, not simply a body part or an emotional center.

The Apostle Paul's Use of Heart

The Apostle Paul uses the concept of the heart to define

salvation: "If you confess with your mouth that Jesus is Lord and believe in your heart that God raised him from the dead, you will be saved." (Rom 10:9) He also employs heart language—foolish hearts—in citing the antithesis of faith, as cited in Romans 1:21 at the beginning of the chapter. This thesis and antithesis uses of heart in Paul's writing implies that the heart is the focal point of spiritual warfare.

Consider Romans 1:21. Normally, we expect an argument to start with a statement of the thesis: The heart is the battlefield over which the question of faith is decided. Because Paul starts, not with the thesis as expected, but the antithesis—foolish hearts—our hearts are not a blank slate that our parents and teachers simply write on. Sin darkens our hearts, making the work of Christ on the cross necessary.

The Problem of Sin

Original sin refers to the rebellion of Adam and Eve in disobeying God to eat of the tree of the knowledge of good and evil (Gen 2:17). This act defined Adam and Eve as lawbreakers and tainted the family tree. While Paul writes about "foolish hearts," there is also a curse: "God gave them up in the lusts of their hearts." (Rom 1:24) "Lusts of their hearts" is rephrased two verses later as "dishonorable passions." (Rom 1:26) Original sin is a heart problem of loving the wrong things.

The heart is accordingly not neutral ground. God's general revelation, often pictured as in Psalm 19 as having an idealized vision of creation, has been rejected. Paul writes: "For his invisible attributes, namely, his eternal power and divine nature, have been clearly perceived, ever since the creation of the world, in the things that have been made." (Rom 1:20) Men and women did not honor God, were ungrateful, and were futile in their thinking (Rom 1:21). Furthermore, "They exchanged the glory of the immortal God for images resembling mortal man and birds and animals and creeping things." (Rom 1:23)

The current fascination with the occult, gender, and recreational drugs are not necessarily innocent obsessions, in part, because they represent confused hearts—hearts not loving the right things. Paul follows these "debased minds" down the slippery slope to their logical conclusion:

> They were filled with all manner of unrighteousness, evil, covetousness, malice. They are full of envy, murder, strife, deceit, maliciousness. They are gossips, slanderers, haters of God, insolent, haughty, boastful, inventors of evil, disobedient to parents, foolish, faithless, heartless, ruthless. (Rom 1:29–31)

While your list of evil acts may not be the same as Paul's, the point is that sin leaves no one untouched whose heart is allowed to gravitate to its own dishonorable passion.

Founding of the Church on Pentecost

The church began with the gift of the Holy Spirit on Pentecost. The Feast of Pentecost marked fifty days after Passover and celebrated the barley harvest (or first fruits; Lev 23). It was a time of joy because the fasting and hunger from the previous winter—the normal situation for most people before the Industrial Revolution—would finally end. In this context, we read:

> When the day of Pentecost arrived, they were all together in one place. And suddenly there came from heaven a sound like a mighty rushing wind, and it filled the entire house where they were sitting. And divided tongues as of fire appeared to them and rested on each one of them. And they were all filled with the Holy Spirit and began to speak in other tongues as the Spirit gave them utterance. (Acts 2:1–4)

Several observations here are important. First, the disciples were "all together in one place." The church's formation was a communal experience. Second, the Holy Spirit is the agent of this transformation "from heaven a sound like a mighty rushing wind" and the one filling each of them. Third, "tongues as of fire" enabled them all to speak in "other tongues."

While the Holy Spirit inaugurates the church collectively, later that same day the Apostle Peter applies the agency of the

Holy Spirit also to individuals, saying: "Repent and be baptized every one of you in the name of Jesus Christ for the forgiveness of your sins, and you will receive the gift of the Holy Spirit." (Acts 2:38) The church provides a forum for repentance, baptism, and communion, but it is the Holy Spirit that is the agent of transformation in the believer following God's special revelation in Jesus Christ.

∞

Holy Spirit,

All praise and honor, power and dominion, truth and justice are yours, because you engendered faith in us and founded the church at Pentecost.

We confess that we have not lived into our salvation or shared it with those in need. Forgive us our selfishness, our pride, and our neglect of your church.

Thank you for Pentecost, for the many spiritual gifts, for your provision and sustenance, and for your presence and protection.

Draw us closer to you ever waking hour. Open our hearts, illumine our thoughts, and strengthen our hands in your service.

In Jesus' precious name, Amen.

∞

Questions
1. How would you describe the biblical heart?

2. What is the role of the heart in salvation, according to the Apostle Paul?
3. How would you describe God's general and special revelations?
4. What is the significance of Pentecost?

Old Testament Images

> *The Spirit of the Lord GOD is upon me,*
> *because the LORD has anointed me*
> *to bring good news to the poor;*
> *he has sent me to bind up the brokenhearted,*
> *to proclaim liberty to the captives,*
> *and the opening of the prison to those who are bound.*
> (Isa 61:1)

*M*any people, many churches, focus on the New Testament and neglect the Old Testament. Yet, the Holy Spirit —the instigator of the church at Pentecost—is alive and well in the Old Testament. Because the Holy Spirit is the agent of God's work in his creation, it is helpful to recognize two distinct Old Testament characteristics: Examples of the Holy Spirit's manifestation and embodiment. I use the term *manifestation of the Holy Spirit* to capture a dynamic pattern of action while the Holy Spirit's embodiment suggests a static miracle, sign, or symbol. Both are important in scripture as God's agency in his creation is described.

Manifestations of the Holy Spirit

The first characteristic of the Holy Spirit is manifestation. The Holy Spirit's footloose nature is manifest in at least two patterns in the Old Testament that display responses to God's invitation of faith. The first manifestation is seen in Abraham's call to faith:

> Now the LORD said to Abram, Go from your country
> and your kindred and your father's house to the land
> that I will show you. And I will make of you a great
> nation, and I will bless you and make your name great,
> so that you will be a blessing. I will bless those who
> bless you, and him who dishonors you I will curse,
> and in you all the families of the earth shall be blessed.
> (Gen 12:1–3)

Abraham must leave behind all sources of security in the ancient world—country, tribe, and family—to respond to God's call. Abraham's faith is displayed in a physical, not verbal, response to this call. God's election becomes obvious in both blessings and curses to prosper and protect Abraham. Evidence of Abraham's election arises in his sharing of God's blessings with others.

While we postmoderns read Abraham's call as the call of an individual, this is a cultural presupposition. Abraham is the male head of his extended family, a communal group that followed him. He also had numerous slaves and a small army of followers (Gen 12:16; 14:14). The name Abraham (father of nations) is more of a title, like king or president (Gen 17:5). Consequently, Abraham's call is more of a communal vision statement.

For those who refuse the invitation of faith, a second manifestation can be seen:

And when all these things come upon you, the blessing and the curse, which I have set before you, and you call them to mind among all the nations where the LORD your God has driven you, and return to the LORD your God, you and your children, and obey his voice in all that I command you today, with all your heart and with all your soul, then the LORD your God will restore your fortunes and have mercy on you, and he will gather you again from all the peoples where the LORD your God has scattered you. (Deut 30:1-3)

Those who refuse faith garner the curse of scattering, an echo of the curse of Cain (Gen 3:14). Here the pattern is collective sin, scattering and enslavement, crying out to the Lord, and the sending of a deliverer. Walter Brueggemann (2016, 59) describes this pattern as the Deuteronomic Cycle.

These two manifestations are repeated throughout scripture and are consistent with Jeffrey Niehaus' (2014, 74) observation: "Earlier biblical portrayals of certain truths can be laconic with more detail provided by later statements or revelations of the same truths." They also represent two responses to God's invitation of faith. All are called; not all respond. One way or the other, through the instrumentality of the Holy Spirit: "To me every knee shall bow, every tongue shall swear allegiance." (Isa 45:23)

Embodiment of the Holy Spirit

The second characteristic of the Holy Spirit is

embodiment. The first person to embody the Holy Spirit is likely Abel, the righteous son of Adam and Eve. Scripture does not actually say that Abel was embodied with the Holy Spirit, but as a shepherd he offered first-born sheep sacrifices that God found acceptable. His brother, Cain, farmed the land and offered fruit that God did not find acceptable—perhaps because the fruit he offered could be taken as a reminder of Adam and Eve's sin (the same word Hebrew and Greek words for fruit are used; Gen 4:2-5). After Cain killed Abel out of jealousy, God cursed Cain to be a wanderer, and Adam and Eve had a third son, Seth, who replaced Abel as the righteous son (Gen 4:25–26).

The genealogy of Genesis 5 ties Seth to Noah. Genealogies in Genesis 10 and 11 tie Noah's righteous son to Abraham. This righteous lineage traces through Abraham's son Isaac and his grandson, Jacob. On coming to faith and later wresting with God, Jacob takes the name, Israel (Gen 28:12-22; 32:24–28) and Jacob's twelve sons form the Nation of Israel. In blessing his sons before his passing, Jacob calls Judah a lion's cub, which is taken as a prophecy of kingly leadership (Gen 49:9–10).

This righteous lineage history lays the groundwork for charismatic leadership where the spiritual legacy of the Holy Spirit takes the form of messianic leaders, those anointed with oil and the laying on of hands. Messianic titles include priests, prophets, and kings. The title *Christ* is a Greek translation of the Hebrew word *messiah*.

The Special Role of Moses

Leadership in Israel went to Joseph bypassing Reuben, Simeon, and Levi (the first-, second-, and third-born sons of Jacob) because of their sin (Gen 34). Moses was of the tribe of Levi, not Judah nor a son of Joseph (Exod 2:1). Nevertheless, God called Moses personally to lead the Nation of Israel out of Egypt (Exod 3:1–10).

Moses embodied the Holy Spirit on account of his personal relationship with God, not his family heritage. As Moses led the Nation of Israel out of Egypt and into the desert, we read:

> And the LORD went before them by day in a pillar of cloud to lead them along the way, and by night in a pillar of fire to give them light, that they might travel by day and by night. (Exod 13:21)

The Holy Spirit is embodied here in a "pillar of cloud" often referred to as the *Shekinah* cloud, where *Shekinah* is a transliteration of the Hebrew word for divine presence. The *Shekinah* cloud is also seen hanging over Mount Sinai with the giving of the law (Exod 19) and over the Tabernacle (Num 9:15), the antecedent of the Temple built in Jerusalem by Solomon (2 Chr 7:1).

The Temple in Jerusalem

The anointing of the Holy Spirit in the Old Testament is given to charismatic leaders and, on one occasion, to seventy leaders of the Nation of Israel (Num 11:25), an antecedent of the founding of the church at Pentecost (Acts 2). The founding of the Temple in Jerusalem started not with the Holy Spirit, but with King David of the tribe of Judah (Ruth 4:12–22) wanting to move the Tabernacle to Jerusalem and replace it with a temple.

God was not altogether pleased with David's idea of building a temple:

> In all places where I have moved with all the people of Israel, did I speak a word with any of the judges of Israel, whom I commanded to shepherd my people Israel, saying, Why have you not built me a house of cedar? (2 Sam 7:7)

Building a temple in the ancient world was a way to control access to the gods and was typically an instrument of nation-building and kingly rule. God forbad David from building a temple because he spent most of his life at war, but conceded that his son, Solomon, could build this temple (2 Sam 7:12–13). God's concession for David's son to build a temple arose as part of his promise to build David's house—a dynasty.

When Solomon built the temple and dedicated it, it was filled with the Shekinah glory of God (2 Chr 7:1). This was the first

Temple of Jerusalem that was later destroyed by the Babylonians (2 Kgs 25:9). A second Temple of Jerusalem was built by the exiles returning from Babylon seventy years later (Ezr 3), but no mention is made of the *Shekinah* cloud.

The idea that God's throne is in heaven suggests that the status of temples as an embodiment of the Holy Spirit has always been problematic (Ps 11:4), and ultimately results in God's abandonment of the temple. This problematic embodiment reaches a highpoint in Jesus' trial before the Sanhedrin when he was charged with destroying the temple and with blasphemy (Mark 14:58–64). Later, with Jesus' crucifixion, the temple veil was torn (Matt 27:51). The Temple in Jerusalem was itself destroyed in AD 70 by the Romans and never rebuilt. This made it impossible for Jews to offer required sacrifices (e.g. Lev 1:1–4). Christians believe that Jesus' death on the cross was the final sacrifice for once and for all (Heb 9).

∞

Almighty Father,

All praise and honor, power and dominion, truth and justice are yours because you have guided us through the ages and invited us to faith for your name's sake.

We confess that we have not always heeded your invitation or even called on your name when we get into trouble.

Do not forget us or subject us to a futility curse (Deut 28:30; Hillers 1964, 78-79).

Thank you for the gift of faith, your Shekinah Cloud, and the fellowship of your spirit and the church. Be ever near.

In the power of your Holy Spirit, guide us through troubled times and guard our hearts when we grow weak. May we always return to you.

In Jesus' precious name, Amen.

∞

Questions
1. What patterns manifest the Holy Spirit in the Old Testament?
2. How would you characterize God's calling of Abraham?
3. Describe the Deuteronomic Cycle.
4. What is the Shekinah Cloud?
5. Why was God ambivalent about the Temple in Jerusalem?

The Holy Spirit in Luke-Acts

*But you will receive power
when the Holy Spirit has come upon you,
and you will be my witnesses
in Jerusalem and in all Judea and Samaria,
and to the end of the earth.*

(Acts 1:8)

*T*he Old Testament name for the Holy Spirit in Genesis 1:2 in Hebrew is *Ruach Elohim*. Ferguson (1996, 17) writes:

> *Ruach* does not connote the idea of divine immateriality (spirit, not matter), although doubtless that is implied in the general biblical perspective. The emphasis is, rather, on his overwhelming energy; indeed, one might almost speak about the violence of God. 'Divine Spirit,' thus denotes 'the energy of life in God.'"

It is translated into the Septuagint Greek interchangeably as *Pneuma Theou* or *Pneuma Kuriou*. In English, these would be Spirit of God and Spirit of the Lord. The Greek *Pneuma Kuriou* is also frequently corresponding to the Hebrew *Ruach YHWH*[1] that also has more metaphorical translations, like breath of God. *Ruach Elohim* is also translated as *Pneuma Poneron* or evil spirit once in Judges and three times in 1 Samuel 16 in reference to King Saul after David had been anointed.

---

1 Jdg 3:10, 11:29, 13:25, 14:6, 19, 15:14, 1 Sam 10:6, 16:13, 19:9, 2 Sam 23:2, 1 Ki 22:24, 2 Kgs 2:16, 2 Chr 18:23, 20:14, Isa 11:2, 40:7, 13, 59:19, 63:14, Ezek 11:5, Hos 13:15, Mic 2:7, and 3:8.

Grieving the Holy Spirit

What is interesting about this list of Old Testament references to the Holy Spirit is that the two primary names for the Holy Spirit in the Book of Acts, *Pneuma Agion* and *Pneuma ta Agion,* do not appear on this list. This latter Greek term for the Holy Spirit does, however, appear twice in the Old Testament. Once in a famous Psalm of David: "Cast me not away from your presence, and take not your Holy Spirit from me." (Ps 51:11) The Hebrew here reads *Ruach Kadeska.* The second time is in Isaiah 63:10, where a variant Hebrew name, *Ruach Kadesho,* is used. The passage cautions God's chosen (Israel in Isaiah's context) not to grieve or quench the Holy Spirit (Finney 1982, 63).

One example of someone obviously grieving the Holy Spirit was King Saul. Saul is described as tall and handsome, but also as superstitious, willful, and impatient (1 Sam 9:2, 15:1–35). By contrast, David was young, ruddy, and handsome, a musician and shepherd, and a man after God's heart (1 Sam 13:14; 16:12). Once the Prophet Samuel anointed David, God sent an evil spirit to torment Saul. Consequently, Saul's servants sought out David to play the lyre to soothe Saul in his affliction and Saul took David as his armor-bearer, a kind of kingly apprenticeship (1 Sam 16:15–21). Later, David becomes Saul's son-in-law.

Being close to King Saul, David observed firsthand the implications of losing the Holy Spirit, which no doubt motivated his prayer (Ps 51:11). The prominence of the Holy Spirit in the foundation of the church and reference to this Old Testament understanding of the Holy Spirit suggest that the story of Saul sheds light on the story of another Saul in the Book of Acts (Acts 8:1).

Something New

This linguistic departure from the more common terms for the Holy Spirit in the Old Testament and the particular passages in view suggest that Luke in the Book of Acts, sees God doing something new. Even in Luke's Gospel, we are told that Jesus receives the Holy Spirit in his baptism prior to Joseph's genealogy that traces his lineage back through Judah, Shem, and Seth to Adam. Luke distances Jesus from this genealogy by distancing Jesus from Joseph's biological parentage (Luke 3:23). Thus, neither the anointing of the righteous lineage (Gen 11), nor the temporary anointing of the Holy Spirit on Moses' elders (Num 11:25) or King Saul (1 Sam 10:6–11) is being claimed or credited. What exactly is new?

At least three things appear new in the Book of Acts as a consequence of the tearing of the curtain in the temple of Jerusalem (Matt 27:51, Mark 15:38, Luke 23:45). First, the disciples were given the mission of being witnesses. Second, the mission was extended geographically from Jerusalem to Judea and Samaria, and to the ends of the earth (Acts 1:8), and, by inference, extends also to Gentiles. Third, the gift of the Holy Spirit is no longer for a season, but forever, again by inference (Acts 2:4). Previously in the Old Testament, the gift of the Holy Spirit was temporary and limited, except perhaps for those of the righteous lineage or those anointed as messiahs.

The Footloose Spirit

The story of King Saul plays out in the Book of Acts in the person of Saul of Tarsus. When the church in Jerusalem appears satisfied to remain in Jerusalem rather than live into its mission (Acts 1:8), Saul is seen ravaging the church and scattering the disciples (Acts 8:1–4). This is like King Saul being tormented and driven to David by an evil spirit (1 Sam 16:15–21).

Once this scattering has been accomplished, we see Saul undergoing a conversion experience and living into his Gentile name, Paul (Acts 9). Paul then becomes one of the church's most celebrated evangelists and joins named and unnamed disciples who carry the church on its mission (Acts 1:8). Thus, we see both the Holy Spirit and its evil twin accomplishing God's work in establishing the church through the person of Saul of Tarsus.

Edmund Clowney (1995, 56) writes:

> The Holy Spirit of God cannot be boxed in by the constraints of human institutions. He is the Creator Spirit, sovereign and omnipotent, who governs all things.

This footloose nature overcomes the usual bounds of established institutions, like the church in Jerusalem, that tend to ossify with time, following familiar pathways rather than following the leadership of God's Holy Spirit. Thus the movement away from Jerusalem to Judea, Samaria, and the ends of the earth is more than an historical experience—it is a revival impulse needed in every generation that is reminiscent of the call of Abraham to leave country, tribe, and family.

Jews and Gentiles

The Holy Spirit anointed Gentiles before acknowledgment of the church confirmed it. We see this in the pouring out of the spirit on the Samaritans (Acts 8:14–17), Philip's witnessing to the Eunuch (Acts 8:26–39), and Peter's vision inviting him to eat both clean and unclean animals before visiting the house of Cornelius, a Roman centurion (Acts 10:22).

Later, at the Council of Jerusalem, in spite of much opposition, the Gospel is provisionally opened to Gentiles (Acts

15:19–20). Consequently, the Gospel reached the farthermost parts of the Roman Empire and beyond within a single generation.

Holy Spirit as Agent of Faith

The purpose of the spirit in evangelism is to identify those called to be the church. The Apostle Peter cited the Prophet Joel (2:28–29) during his sermon on the Day of Pentecost:

> And in the last days it shall be, God declares, that I will pour out my Spirit on all flesh, and your sons and your daughters shall prophesy, and your young men shall see visions, and your old men shall dream dreams; even on my male servants and female servants in those days I will pour out my Spirit, and they shall prophesy. (Acts 2:17–18)

In citing this passage in Joel, Peter clearly believes he is living in the "last days," a sentiment held by many today. Peter then describes the path to faith: "Repent and be baptized every one of you in the name of Jesus Christ for the forgiveness of your sins, and you will receive the gift of the Holy Spirit." (Acts 2:38) This suggests that the Holy Spirit is both the sign and seal of faith, and with it, salvation. In some sense, the Apostle John's term for the Holy Spirit, the Paraclete, or in English, the comforter, embodies both ideas.

∞

Holy Father,

All praise and honor, power and dominion, truth and justice are yours because you called the church into being from the nations and blessed it with your Holy Spirit that we might be witnesses among those who are sick and dying.

Forgive us for forsaking your call and not sharing your blessings with those in dire need.

Thank you for sustenance, gifting, and protection of your Holy Spirit.

In the power of your Holy Spirit, open our hearts, illumine our minds, and strengthen our hands in your service.

In Jesus' precious name, Amen.

∞

Questions
1. What is your favorite name for the Holy Spirit?
2. What does it mean to grieve the Holy Spirit?
3. What is special about the Greek words that are used in the Book of Acts to describe the Holy Spirit?
4. How does King Saul's experience of the Holy Spirit inform the Book of Acts?
5. What is new in the Book of Acts and why?

The Church in Paul's Writing

> *Having been forbidden by the Holy Spirit*
> *to speak the word in Asia. ...*
> *And a vision appeared to Paul in the night:*
> *a man of Macedonia was standing there,*
> *urging him and saying, come over to Macedonia*
> *and help us."*
> (Acts 16:6–9)

*T*he manifestation of the Holy Spirit in the Apostle Paul's writing is most obvious in his calling as an evangelist to the Gentiles (Rom 11:13). Yet more than any other author in the New Testament, Paul worked to embody the Holy Spirit to establish churches, mentor its leaders, and explain the Gospel in deeply theological terms. In his evangelism and leadership, Paul exhibits the heart of a pastor, living out holy and inclusive leadership, yet remaining sensitive to the nudges of the Holy Spirit.

Set Apart for Leadership

More than any others, Paul mentored church leaders. Listen to Paul's words to Timothy concerning his call to leadership in the church:

> Now in a great house there are not only vessels of gold and silver but also of wood and clay, some for honorable use, some for dishonorable. Therefore, if anyone cleanses himself from what is dishonorable, he will be a vessel for honorable use, set apart as holy, useful to the master of the house, ready for every good work. So

flee youthful passions and pursue righteousness, faith, love, and peace, along with those who call on the Lord from a pure heart. (2 Tim 2:20–22)

Here Paul compares the church to a "great house," presumably of someone wealthy enough to have "vessels of gold and silver." A leader is someone "set apart as holy" and "ready for every good work" who flees "youthful passions" and pursues "righteousness, faith, love, and peace" having a "pure heart." Here we see both a call to holiness and to godliness (Bridges 1996, 7).

Clearly, Paul's sees a Christian leader in the church as someone created in the image of God himself and willing to live into that image. Much like in Paul's discussion of the fruits of the spirit— "love, joy, peace, patience, kindness, goodness, faithfulness, gentleness, self-control" (Gal 5:22–23), we hear an echo of God's own attributes revealed to Moses on Mount Sinai: "The LORD, the LORD, a God merciful and gracious, slow to anger, and abounding in steadfast love and faithfulness." (Exod 34:6) Exhibiting these attributes, we see Paul's image for the church reflected in a holy heart:

Or do you not know that your body is a temple of the Holy Spirit within you, whom you have from God? You are not your own, for you were bought with a price. So glorify God in your body. (1 Cor 6:19–20)

Paul envisions the church as an outward manifestation of an

inward reality. The Cherubim guard God's temple, which Niehaus (2014, 122–123) cites as evidence that believers—as temples of the Holy Spirit—are also protected by guardian angels.

Church as an Agency of the Holy Spirit

The agency of the Holy Spirit in founding and sustaining the church is highlighted in the Apostle Paul's term for the church (Thompson 2014, 25). He refers to the church as the "called out ones of God" in Greek (e.g. 1 Cor 1:2). When those called by God get together, that is the church. The church is not a building or club; it is composed only of those called out by God himself. Because only God truly knows who he has called, the Westminster Confession of faith disguises the visible church we see from the invisible church seen only by God (PCUSA 1999, 6.140). Jesus himself makes this distinction in his parable of the wheat and the tares (Matt 13:24–30).

The authority of the church and of the Bible rests on the agency of the Holy Spirit. This authority is often physically manifested in the laying on of hands in coming to faith (e.g. Acts 8:17), during ordination (e.g. Num 27:18; 1 Tim 5:22), and in healing (e.g. Luke 4:40), echoing the practice of the patriarchs in passing on the righteous lineage of God. Oftentimes, the Holy Spirit acts independently of the church through visions and through the reading of scripture to bring surprising people to faith, like the Apostle Paul.

Inclusive Leadership

Paul's commitment to theological discourse is especially obvious in his promotion of inclusive leadership. Consider Paul's sermon on Mars Hill: "The times of ignorance God overlooked, but now he commands all people (*anthropois*) everywhere to repent." (Acts 17:30) Moments after saying that "all people everywhere" must repent to an audience of Greek philosophers in their most sacred and scholarly location, Paul is seen evangelizing a woman: "But some men joined him and believed, among whom also were Dionysius the Areopagite and a woman named Damaris and others with them." (Acts 17:34) So while *anthropois* is gender ambiguous (plural male included women in common use) in this context, Paul's actions suggests that his intent is inclusive. Hence, the English translation reads all people, not all men.

If Paul were a typical misogynist, he would not speak to any women about the Gospel. Yet Paul's strongest support came from the church that he established in the city of Phillippi, where Roman soldiers went to retire. Listen to how this church came into being:

> And on the Sabbath day we went outside the gate to the riverside, where we supposed there was a place of prayer, and we sat down and spoke to the women who had come together. One who heard us was a woman named Lydia, from the city of Thyatira, a seller of purple goods, who was a worshiper of God. The Lord opened her heart to pay attention to what was said by Paul. (Acts 16:13–14)

Paul lived out his statement of "all people everywhere," which is why he evangelized women and was able to write: "There is neither Jew nor Greek, there is neither slave nor free, there is no male and female, for you are all one in Christ Jesus." (Gal 3:28) Who else could persuasively argue with a slaveholder that his runaway slave should be considered a brother in Christ? (Phlm 1:16)

Paul's commitment to theological discourse is usually touted in his letter to the church at Rome, where he employs a highly philosophical, nurture-nature argument to advance the Gospel. Yet, the depth of Paul's commitment to inclusive leadership in mentoring a young Timothy, forgiving Onesimus, and evangelizing women like Lydia demonstrates more clearly that Paul took his theology to heart, a spirituality of lived theology (Chan 1998,16). One has to wonder whether Paul's inclusive leadership theology, far from being incidental, revealed a key strategy in his evangelism founded on Joel's Prophecy (Joel

2:28–29).

∞

Beloved Lord Jesus,

All praise and honor, power and dominion, truth and justice are yours because you teach us the errors of our ways and draw us closer to you in spite of vast differences in time, space, and moral distance.

Forgive us for being slow learners that do not understand or want to understand your will for our lives.

Thank you for the ministry of devout pastors, the inspiration of reasoned prophets, and the arguments of learned evangelists that draw us to you and build up your church.

In the power your Holy Spirit, open our hearts, illumine our thoughts, and strengthen our hands in your service.

In the name of the Father, the Son, and the Holy Spirit, Amen.

∞

Questions
1. Why is mentoring important to Paul?
2. Why is inclusive leadership a theological issue?
3. Who was Lydia? Who was Onesimus? Who was Timothy?
4. What was Paul's vision of the church?
5. Why was Paul's sermon on Mars Hill important?

The Spirit in John-Revelation

> *But the Helper, the Holy Spirit,*
> *whom the Father will send in my name,*
> *he will teach you all things and bring to your remembrance*
> *all that I have said to you.*
> *(John 14:26)*

f the Holy Spirit instigated external events in church history for Luke and the Holy Spirit inspired internal faith and community life for Paul, the Holy Spirit worked miraculously through custom, covenants, and visions for John in forming the church. John gives us several well-known, genderless titles for God—The I AM, the Alpha and Omega, and the Almighty—that express God's power, majesty, and divine agency (Rev 1:8). These titles are not specifically used to describe the Holy Spirit, but they address God in the person of the Holy Spirit most aptly. John casts the most complete vision of the New Testament church.

The Holy Spirit in John's Gospel

John's Gospel uses the term Holy Spirit only three times. In the first context, John the Baptist identifies Jesus as the one who baptizes with his Holy Spirit (John 1:33). In the second, John gives an outline of the Holy Spirit's job description, as cited above. In the final context, Jesus commissions the disciples as apostles—"As the Father has sent me, even so I am sending you"—and grants them the Holy Spirit (John 20:21–22). In the Greek, an apostle is literally one who is sent.

The first and the final use of the Holy Spirit is in divine commissioning. The second use is interesting to us here because it provides an interpretative key. Jesus' teaching is not forgotten because the task of the Holy Spirit, the Paraclete, is specifically to teach and help the disciples remember Jesus' teaching (John 14:26). This is a very personal job description for the Holy Spirit, something not provided by other biblical authors. The Holy Spirit is not just an impersonal force or invisible agent (breath of God) sent by God—everyone knows the name and nudge of their tutor.

The Holy Spirit in Revelation

The term Holy Spirit does not appear in Revelation but the book refers to the Spirit and to angels repeatedly in the context of offering advice to the church. John uses two specific phrases to identify seven churches in the second and third chapters of Revelation. First, he says: "To the angel of the church in" (Rev 2:1, 2:8, 2:12, 2:18, 3:1, 3:7, 3:14). Closely following this phrase, he repeats: "Hear what the Spirit says to the churches" (Rev 2:7, 2:11, 2:17, 2:29, 3:6, 3:13, 3:22). The churches mentioned are Ephesus, Smyrna, Pergamum, Thyatira, Sardis, Philadelphia, and

Laodicea, respectively. What follows after this stylistic language is prophecy offering both praise and rebuke to churches in Asia Minor. This series of exhortations models the *Paraclete* mentioned in John's Gospel who is at work in the daily life of the churches.

Another clear prophecy to the church is:

> Then the voice that I had heard from heaven spoke to me again, saying, go, take the scroll that is open in the hand of the angel who is standing on the sea and on the land. So I went to the angel and told him to give me the little scroll. And he said to me, take and eat it; it will make your stomach bitter, but in your mouth it will be sweet as honey. And I took the little scroll from the hand of the angel and ate it. It was sweet as honey in my mouth, but when I had eaten it my stomach was made bitter. And I was told, you must again prophesy about many peoples and nations and languages and kings. (Rev 10:8–11)

While this passage clearly echoes language in Ezekiel 3:1–3, the voice from heaven sounds like the avian metaphor for the Holy Spirit (Gen 1:2). In this vision, prophecy is shown to be illuminating (or interpreting) scripture, which is the Old Testament role of the prophet. That is, drawing attention to God's covenantal obligations rather than providing new revelation (Ferguson 1997, 214). This vision is emphatic because it references two sources of authority: The voice from heaven and a giant angel with one foot on land and the other on the sea.

The Apostle John in Revelation makes allusion to a vast array of Old Testament scripture, stories, and covenants, more than any other book in the New Testament. However, a recurring theme is to usher us into the throne room of God—the ultimate appeal to authority—and to observe proper worship:

> Let us rejoice and exult and give him the glory, for the marriage of the Lamb has come, and his Bride has made herself ready; it was granted her to clothe herself with fine linen, bright and pure—for the fine linen is the righteous deeds of the saints. (Rev 19:7–8)

Most curious is to see "fine linen" compared with "the righteous deeds of the saints." There is a sense in this abrupt comparison that the usual focus in high and mighty worship on fancy clothes, as in a kingly coronation, is being almost ridiculed in casual comparison here. Perhaps, proper worship requires a pure heart and righteous deeds, not fancy linen.

∞

Almighty Father,

All praise and honor, power and dominion, truth and justice are yours because you guide your church with prophets, visions, and scripture to understand your will for us.

Forgive us for our preoccupation with things of earth rather than things of heaven.

Thank you for the witness of the saints, the sagacity of scripture, and the example of godly friends that point us to you.

In the power of your Holy Spirit, walk with us each and every day that we might not stumble and might rather become witnesses of your love to those around us.

In Jesus' precious name, Amen.

∞

Questions
1. What is your favorite title for God?
2. What are the three citations that the Apostle John uses for the Holy Spirit in his Gospel?
3. What is interesting about John's testimony to the seven churches?
4. What is the Paraclete's role?

THE POSTMODERN DILEMMA

Synopsis

A survey of the challenges facing the church today shows that challenges to the church posed in the modern era lack philosophical merit. The church needs to articulate its message attending to both the heart and the mind. Church growth in the Global South is most successful when its missionaries overcome the challenge of social and economic distance. The rise of materialism in the postmodern era is a more fundamental challenge to the church because it precludes the existence of God by definition and reinforces the current crisis of authority. However, the postmodern challenge is ultimately less onerous because the church's description of the human condition rings truer than the alternatives presented.

Modern Challenges to the Church

Whatever is true, whatever is honorable,
whatever is just, whatever is pure,
whatever is lovely, whatever is commendable,
if there is any excellence, if there is anything worthy of praise,
think about these things.

(Phil 4:8)

*T*he defining problem facing the church over the past two centuries has been responding to the Enlightenment. The development of science applied first in agriculture and later in manufacturing, medicine, and other fields helped convert rural agricultural societies into urban industrial and later service-oriented societies. The natural world began to appear so much better that the supernatural aspects of the Bible came into question. The vast improvements in the material status of ordinary people led many to believe that they no longer needed to believe in or depend on God.

The American church responded to these Enlightenment changes in two ways. Evangelicals continued to believe the Bible needed to be trusted in a literal sense. Liberals continued to adhere to biblical teaching and to claim the authority of scripture, but only up to the point of things that could be naturally explained.

They were like Thomas Jefferson who redacted his Bible to scratch out miracles and supernatural events that he could not believe. Unfortunately, neither evangelicals nor liberals seriously engaged the philosophical questions posed by atheists, implicitly suggesting that the criticism was apt.

Applying the Scientific Method to Problem Definition

In areas of great uncertainty, it is helpful to apply the scientific method to organizing one's thoughts (e.g. Mahan, Troxell, and Allen).

Johnson (1986, 15) outlines the scientific method with these steps: Problem definition, Observation, Analysis, Decision, Execution and Responsibility bearing. In class, he later added a felt need as the preliminary step. In my experience as a government researcher, the key step in the scientific method is the movement from a felt need to a problem definition.

Too frequently, leaders have jumped from a felt need to advocating a favorite prescription without bothering to define the problem or undertaking the other steps in the scientific method. This methodological deficiency is expensive and, when it fails, motivates advocacy of another prescription or a personnel change. In the process, resources are wasted, the problem goes unsolved, and observers become discouraged.

The U.S. church has felt the need to stem the declining membership and financial resources, the erosion of faith among our youth, and the loss of church influence in society. How do we translate this felt need into a definition of the problem facing the church?

Criticism During the Modern and Postmodern Eras

Plantinga (2000, 136-142) observes that atheist philosophers have criticized Christian belief as irrational but not in the usual sense—Nietzsche, for example, referred to Christianity as a slave religion. Freud described Christianity as "wish-fulfillment" and as an illusion serving not a rational purpose, but serving psychological purposes. Marx describes religion as "the opium of the people," which suggests a type of cognitive dysfunction.

Plantinga (2000, 151) concludes:

> When Freud and Marx say that Christian belief
> or theistic belief or even perhaps religious belief
> in general is irrational, the basic idea is that belief

of this sort is not among the proper deliverances of our rational faculties.

Plantinga (2000, 153-154, 163) accordingly concludes that the real criticism of "Christian belief, whether true or false, is at any rate without warrant." Plantinga's strategy in analyzing the atheist complaints accordingly is to discuss what they are not saying—not complaining about evidence, not complaining about rationality in the usual sense, not offering evidence that God does not exist—to eliminate the non-issues.

What remains as their complaint is a twist on rationality—actually more of a rant—you must be on drugs or out of your mind—which is not a serious philosophical complaint except for the fact that so many people repeat it.

More recent critics are even less formal in their criticism. Ganssle (2009, 4) observes that recent atheists do not bother to validate their hypotheses and maintain a deliberate strategy of innuendo that he describes as a Nietzschean genealogy—a genealogy given not to prove that one's family includes royalty, but to discredit the family (Ganssle 2009, 136-137). This pattern of arguing dysfunction and innuendo makes it important to clarify what proper mental function looks like.

A Model of Proper Mental Function

In outlining a proper mental function, Plantinga (2000, xi) defines the concept of warrant:

> Warrant is intimately connected with proper [mental] function. More fully, a belief has warrant if it is produced by cognitive process or faculties that are functioning properly, in a cognitive environment that is propitious for the exercise of cognitive powers, according to a design plan that is successfully aimed at the production of true belief.

He goes on to explain:

> A belief has warrant only if it is produced by cognitive faculties that are functioning properly, subject to no disorder or dysfunction—construed as including absence of impedance as well as pathology. (Plantinga 2000, 153-154)

We accordingly care a lot about the mental state of society when it comes to faith, as cited above in Philippians 4:8.

If atheist criticisms are simply slander, not philosophically-warranted criticism, then the church need not anguish over such philosophical dust bunnies. In a philosophical debate where it has already been demonstrated that the existence of God can neither be logically proved nor disproved, the real question is who tells the most credible story as to how the world works.

Given this premise, the Christian message best explains the human condition and the role of God—if anyone is actually paying attention. In the media-rich environment where we live, attention spans are short, disinformation is rampant, and the still-small voice of God is being drowned out by busyness and temptations. Even on Sunday morning in church, it is not clear that people are tuned in. Consequently, while atheists' criticisms have received the most attention, it is not clear that they pose the most pressing concern.

If the church's mission is to assure good formation of our members, especially young people, then proper mental function is clearly part of this formation. Still, formation requires both clear thinking and dedicated feelings, while proper mental function focuses narrowly on the first part—cognitive clarity. In formation, one must also learn to love the good, an idea extending beyond cognitive function to matters of the heart. Consequently, the problem facing the church appears to be finding a proper balance between heart and mind in ministry while avoiding distractions and being careful to respond to criticism in a timely manner.

∞

Almighty and ever-present Father,

All praise and honor, power and dominion, truth and justice are yours because you created us and sent Christ to die for our sins. May your name be lifted up over the shouting and evil of this world.

Forgive us for our inattention, our sin in the presence of blessings, and our unwillingness to hear your still-small voice. May your name be lifted up in spite of our stopped-up ears.

Thank you for the gift of your Holy Spirit, who provisions us, comforts us, and points us to your word when we need it most.

In the power of your Holy Spirit, open our hearts, illumine our thoughts, and strengthen our hands in your service,

In Jesus' precious name, Amen.

∞

Questions
1. What are the two most prominent responses to the Enlightenment?
2. What are the steps in the scientific method? Which step is critical?
3. What is the church's felt need?
4. How does Plantinga describe the chief criticism of atheists?
5. What is proper mental function and why do we care?

Unity of Heart and Mind

The LORD saw that
the wickedness of man was great in the earth,
and that every intention of the thoughts of his heart
was only evil continually.
(Gen 6:5)

*T*have discussed the defining problem and primary philosophical criticisms of the church over the past two centuries. How do we find proper balance between heart and mind in ministry?

Let's start by recognizing that proper mental function—cognitive clarity—is an insufficient condition for faith. The world is full of data, but not all information has value. Information has value when we find it useful, which is another way of saying we respond emotionally to it. Faith can only be genuine when both the heart and the mind are engaged, which implies that we need to care about faith and see its importance.

Hebrew and Greek Anthropology

This interdependence between thinking and emotion has been described as Hebrew anthropology, while in Greek anthropology, thinking and emotion are separate (e.g. Benner 1992, 11). Since the modern era, professionals have been taught to distinguish facts (observations) from values (feelings), which is an application of Greek anthropology.

Hebrew anthropology is assumed throughout the Bible. In Genesis 6:5, cited at the beginning of the chapter, we read the phrase "every intention of the thoughts of his heart." In Greek thinking, thoughts reside in our heads, not our hearts, but in Hebrew thinking, head and heart are interdependent. What Greek would talk about "the thoughts and attitudes of the heart?" (Heb 4:12) Even more interesting, the wickedness of man—original sin—pollutes not only heart and mind, but also the will—intention. No part of our person goes untouched by sin.

Emotions not Disembodied

The interdependence of heart and mind in Hebrew anthropology conflicts with the cultural presumption today that emotions arise primarily out of physiology. This is a materialistic presumption. While placing one's hand on a stove or in a fire elicits a physiological response and emotions accompany that response, more normally we get emotional about things that are important to us.

This relationship between things important to us and our emotional response is known as the cognitive theory of emotions (Elliott 2006, 46-47). Because God gets angry primarily when we sin or display a hardened heart, the Bible depicts God as adhering to the cognitive theory of emotions (Gen 6:6; Mark 3:1–6). In this sense, God is emotionally intelligent and does not get randomly angry or display bad behavior like other gods of the Ancient Near East. "The God of Genesis is not capricious, impulsive, or shortsighted" (Niehaus 2014, 162).

Implications for Formation of Faith

Hebrew anthropology has serious implications for formation of faith because apologetics has traditionally focused narrowly on explaining the faith without considering the emotional component. The Apostle Peter writes:

> In your hearts honor Christ the Lord as holy, always being prepared to make a defense to anyone who asks you for a reason for the hope that is in you; yet do it with gentleness and respect. (1 Pet 3:15)

While this passage is widely quoted in apologetic discussions, note the heart reference and that the rest of the epistle focuses on lifestyle evangelism. Lifestyle evangelism focuses on living a life that commends the Gospel. This lifestyle naturally blends heart and mind in activities like hospitality and service, but must also include reflection and prayer.

While this subject of heart and mind is timely, it is not new. Theologian Jonathan Edwards (2009, 13), writing in 1746 about the effects of the Great Awakening, noted that both head and heart were necessarily involved in effective discipling. Thus, he coined the phrase "holy affections" to distinguish the marks of the work of the Spirit from other works and associated these holy affections directly with scripture. Holy affections lead us to love the good and hate the bad.

Postmodern Tendencies

While the Great Awakening occurred during the Age of Reason (1685–1815) when cognitive discourse dominated ecclesiological debate, postmoderns often lead with emotions. The poster-child of postmodernism is the narcissist, who crashes and burns while chasing their emotions and ignoring sound advice and reason.

Following this trend, the postmodern church is lite on theology and heavy on emotion. Even the typical Bible study today rarely focuses on a reading a good book, but rather on watching a good video where time for reflection never goes beyond "what it means to me" style discussions. While reader interpretations ("what it means to me") are part of any hermeneutical exercise, it is important first to understand author intent and the context of scripture (Vanhoozer 1998, 25). A good Calvinist also would want to read the text in the original Hebrew and Greek to avoid translation biases.

Given the cultural tendencies of our time, balance between heart and mind can only be achieved with a greater focus on why we care about faith. Loving the good matters because indifference leads to bad outcomes. Human rights and democracy matter more than ethnic/ gender rights and privileges because we have been created equal before God. Without faith, priorities change and the fruits of faith do not automatically survive.

∞

Blessed Lord Jesus,

All glory and honor, power and dominion, truth and justice are yours because through your Holy Spirit, you stretch both our hearts and our minds to understand your scripture and to reach out to those around us.

Forgive us for neglecting your word and disrespecting the people that you put in our lives. Give us the strength to confess our sin and to make recompense for those we hurt.

Thank you for the gift of the scriptures and the example of the saints in following your example.

In the power of your Holy Spirit, bind our hearts and minds together in faith that we might grow in the fellowship of the church to serve others and honor your name.

In your precious name, Amen.

Questions
1. Why is cognitive clarity a precondition, but insufficient for faith?
2. How do Hebrew and Greek anthropology differ?
3. What is the cognitive theory of emotion?
4. What was the dominant tendency in the Age of Reason? What about now?

Collecting Some Data

> *But some men came down from Judea*
> *and were teaching the brothers,*
> *unless you are circumcised according to the custom of Moses,*
> *you cannot be saved. And after Paul*
> *and Barnabas had no small dissension*
> *and debate with them,*
> *Paul and Barnabas and some of the others*
> *were appointed to go up to Jerusalem*
> *to the apostles and the elders*
> *about this question.*
> (Acts 15:1–2)

*H*aving sketched out a problem definition, the scientific method prescribes collecting data. Following Glenn Johnson (1986, 15), one should expect to return to the problem definition as data are collected and this new information suggests clarification of the problem definition. Johnson saw this feedback loop as an important philosophical contribution of the postmodern era.

The Jerusalem Council

One might describe the Jerusalem Council discussion of the circumcision of Gentiles cited above as an example of such a feedback loop in the history of the church. It is interesting that it was Peter, not Paul, who presented the logic of this debate:

And God, who knows the heart, bore witness to

them [the Gentile believers], by giving them the Holy
Spirit just as he did to us, and he made no distinction
between us and them, having cleansed their hearts by
faith. (Acts 15:8–9)

Peter points to the sovereign act of the Holy Spirit to bring Gentiles

to faith. He does not argue that it will increase membership nor

does he commend Paul for his role in this evangelistic effort.

Peter talked neither of programs nor of plans; rather, he looked

to what the Holy Spirit was doing in the midst of the church.

The phrase, "cleansed their heart by faith," echoes the

prophecy of Jeremiah: "Circumcise yourselves to the LORD;

remove the foreskin of your hearts." (Jer 4:4) Peter's insight

here is no doubt the result of prayer and reflection on the rite of

circumcision. We can, of course, advance God's work in our lives

by being open to spiritual formation, but we see no mention of

this aspect of faith in Peter's remarks.

The Holy Spirit's Work Today

Following Peter's logic, where do we see the Holy Spirit

at work in the world churches today? While we cannot know

with precision where the Holy Spirit is at work, statistics on the

number of Christians and where they live show some definite

trends.

Researchers at the Center for the Study of Global

Christianity at Gordon-Conwell Theological Seminary observed in 2021:

> The concept of who a missionary is has evolved since the beginning of the twentieth century, making it much more difficult to assess how many missionaries there are in the world. The proportion of long-term missionaries from the Global North is on the decline (227,000 sent in 2021, which is 53 percent of the total of 430,000, down from 88 percent of the total in 1970). Since the 1980s and 1990s there has been a dramatic explosion of the number of short-term missionaries, particularly youth, who spend as little as a week outside their own cultural context. (Zurlo, Johnson, and Crossing 2021, 16-17)

If the number of missionaries sent is a barometer of religious fervor, then these statistics suggest that the Global North is being displaced as the center of Christian activity by the Global South. This fervor likewise reflects the number of Christians in these regions:

> In 2021 a total of 1.7 billion Christians (67 percent) are found in the Global South. Projecting religious affiliation at the country level, it is probable that by 2050 there will be 2.6 billion Christians (77 percent) in the Global South. (Zurlo, Johnson, and Crossing 2021, 19)

The Christian groups accounting for these trends are obvious:

> The Pentecostal/Charismatic movement is one of the fastest-growing trends in World Christianity today . . . This movement grew from 58 million in 1970 to 656 million in 2021. The Global South is home to 86 percent of all Pentecostals/Charismatics in the world.

Without the growth among Pentecostals and Charismatics, the number of Christians in the world would have been flat to declining over the past century. If we take these statistics as a measure of body temperature, we see definite tension between the embodied and the footloose manifestations of the Holy Spirit in our time.

∞

Almighty Father,

All praise and honor, power and dominion, truth and justice are yours because you seek us out and bless us where we work and live, not leaving us to our own devices. Draw us closer to you day by day.

Forgive us when we neglect your nudges and drown out your still, small voice with music and activities of our own choosing. Draw us closer to you day by day.

Thank you for your model of forgiveness in Jesus Christ, who lived a righteous life, died on the cross for our sins, and rose again that we might be forgiven and participate in everlasting life. Draw us closer to you day by day.

In the power of your Holy Spirit, offer us not only consolation but also transformation (Rom 12:1–2) that we might not be content to live in old bodies of death but grow to life in new bodies of life in you. Open our hearts; illumine our thoughts; strengthen our hands in your service.

In Jesus' precious name, Amen.

∞

Questions
1. What is a feedback loop in the scientific method?
2. What was the role of the Holy Spirit in accepting Gentile converts into the church?
3. What is heart circumcision?
4. Where is the church growing most rapidly today?

Analyzing the Data

*If you pay attention to the one
who wears the fine clothing and say,
You sit here in a good place, while you say to the poor man,
You stand over there, or, Sit down at my feet,
have you not then made distinctions among yourselves
and become judges with evil thoughts?*
(Jas 2:3–4)

*T*he North-South distinction in missions highlights the problem in the church with social and economic distance that also shows in distinctions among the denominations. The response to the modern-day Pentecostal movement is typical.

The Pentecostal revival dates back to the Azuza Street (Los Angles, California) revival:

> On the evening of April 9, 1906, Seymour and seven other men were waiting before the Lord when suddenly, as though hit by a bolt of lightning, they were knocked from their chairs to the floor. The seven men with Seymour began to speak in diverse kinds of tongues magnifying God. The shouts were so fervent and loud that news spread quickly of the unusual events on Bonnie Brae Street. A few days later Seymour finally received the Holy Spirit. (PCG 2020, 87)

William Joseph Seymour (1870–1922) was African-American.

From the beginning, the Pentecostal movement was multiracial and multiethnic, focused on the working classes, and admitted anyone with a call to minister, preach, and evangelize. From the beginning, this included young people and women. By contrast, Presbyterians are majority white, focus on professionals, and limit ministry primarily to those seminary trained.

Pentecostals and Social Distance

Social distance is a term used by sociologists to denote differences in class, ethnicity, race, or gender. The Pentecostal movement spread quickly in the Global South in part because Pentecostals shared the same social position as those they evangelized. This is an important point in Africa because Muslim missionaries often depict Christianity as a "white man's religion." This slander is ironic because many of the early Christian theologians, such as Augustine, were African until Islam swept through North Africa in the seventh century. Nevertheless, husband-wife African American and Hispanic Pentecostal missionary teams could easily dismiss such arguments while missionaries from mainline protestant denominations find such criticism more challenging.

Social Distance and Fervor

The challenge of social distance is a problem primarily when combined with a decline in religious fervor. Ministry across economic and social classes is not just a problem in overseas missions. It is a factor in virtually all ministry outreach efforts where such differences exist.

The biblical answer to the problem of social and economic distance is to treat the church as an extended family (Hellerman 2001, 2). The Apostle Paul writes:

> In Christ Jesus you are all sons of God, through faith. . . . There is neither Jew nor Greek, there is neither slave nor free, there is no male and female, for you are all one in Christ Jesus. And if you are Christ's, then you are Abraham's offspring, heirs according to promise. (Gal 3:26–29)

As sons and daughters of God through Jesus Christ, the New Testament refers to fellow Christians as brothers and sisters in Christ who are recipients of the promises that God made to Abraham.

Social distance becomes an issue of fervor because we are obligated to support family members in need. Whose needs will we meet and to what extent? It is easier to ignore poverty when it is hidden from view, which is hard to do when a poor brother or sister is a member of your church or a mission partner.

An Illustration of Social Distance

When I was in seminary several years ago, my parents, who attended a Presbyterian Church (USA), hosted two pastors from Kenya who were mission partners of their church. Over dinner several awkward moments arose. When asked about their journey of faith, one said that when he came to Christ he stopped beating his wife. When asked where they attended seminary, a deathly silence followed. When the subject of homosexuality came up, we learned that their Presbytery had broken communion with ours that week in spite of our financial support.

Obviously, many factors come to play in exacerbating social distance.

Factors Influencing Social Distance

Social and economic distance is more than a hypothetical issue for Christians. Declining religious fervor in the Global North, the flip side of secularization of the church, has recently been compounded by the declines in standards of living, fertility, and life expectancy among the majority of Americans. Increasing Christianization of the Global South has been accompanied by rapid urbanization and the consequent loss of community suffered by many people, a situation analogous to the situation of first century Christians.

The contrast between the Global North and Global South provides an interesting mirror for self-reflection. Because urbanization has run its course in the Global North, part of the problem with secularization may be simply being too settled and not feeling a need to reach out to others. This might seem to be an ironic observation as standards of living fall in the Global North (an unsettling development), but spiritual lethargy is also evident in greater drug use, gender confusion, inattention to educational opportunities, and political polarization.

If we are one in Christ, what are we when we ignore Christ?

∞

Loving Father,

All praise and honor, power and dominion, truth and justice are yours because you brought us together and called us to be a people, your people (1 Pet 2:9–10). Unify us in Christ.

Forgive our inattention, our complacency, our

lethargy in the face of challenges. Unify us in Christ.

Thank you for the many blessings in this life: health, family, homes, and medical plans. Unify us in you, not these other things.

In the power of your Holy Spirit, open our eyes and unstop our ears as the fire of self-destruction approaches. May we feel the heat before we are burned, and all that is precious to us is swept away.

In Jesus' precious name, Amen.

∞

Questions
1. How would you describe social and economic distance?
2. What is one reason that the Pentecostal movement has spread rapidly in the Global South?
3. What is the biblical answer to social and economic distance?
4. What measure of religious fervor can we see at work in the world today?

Defining the Church

For where two or three are gathered in my name,
there am I among them.
(Matt 18:20)

*T*he church is not easily defined. The Apostle Paul's term *ecclesia* (1 Cor 1:2), which means *called out ones,* remains helpful because it describes an organic institution defined primarily by its call, not by its institutional structure. On Pentecost when the church was born, the defining characteristic of those called was the tongues of fire (Acts 2:3) that rested on their head. At seminary, we used to describe those truly tuned into their work as having "their hair on fire for the Lord," an obvious allusion to the Pentecost experience.

The Old Testament description of a church, *kahal* (BDB 8447), means assembly, convocation, congregation. In Deuteronomy, we read: "Gather the people to me, that I may let them hear my words" (Deut 4:10). The context here offers a purpose—hear my words—and a particular time suggesting the ecclesia is even here not a random group or group defined by a particular place as in a temple. This purpose highlights the role of worship in the church.

While this is obviously not a comprehensive review

of the Old Testament-New Testament contrast in view of the church, it highlights the contrast between the footloose and embodied interpretations of the work of the Holy Spirit in the church.

The Question of Mission

As a practical matter, church leaders often struggle to articulate their corporate mission, especially as they approach the calling of pastors. The usual strategy is to plan a leadership retreat and brainstorm a mission statement that ends up plastered on business cards, stationary, and miscellaneous swag. The problem with the MBA approach to discerning a church call is it focuses on group process rather than observing movement of the spirit within the life of the church.

In my work as a hospital chaplain, I met a troubled woman—a paraplegic—in the emergency department. When I asked her about scripture or perhaps a Bible story that she enjoyed, she talked about the story of Joseph, whose brothers threw him in a pit and later sold him as a slave (Gen 37). As a paraplegic, this woman had been abused by her family even as they lived off of her government transfer payments. This woman's life story was a direct analogy to the story of Joseph, which for her was a rehearsal story, a story from the past with current significance (Savage 1996, 84–89).

My story of the paraplegic highlights one method for discerning God's call on a particular church. What passage of scripture best describes significant work or events in the life of the church? A campus church might mirror the mentoring work, for example, of Barnabas who encouraged the Apostle Paul (Acts 4:36; 9:27). An inner-city church might relate to the story of the woman at the well (John 4). A house church in China might relate to the story of Abigail, who saved her foolish husband's life by offering hospitality to David (1 Sam 25). Understanding a parallel biblical story can suggest additional elements that would be helpful in the current context.

Because churches often combine a collection of ministries, each of the ministries may have its own unique calling much like a vegetable stand in a farmer's market: a market with various types of produce. The call of the wider church may lie in helping these ministries define their mission and resource their work.

Signs of the Times

Two historical trends in the church have come together in recent years to complicate arriving at a proper definition of the church (and a proper sense of Christian identity) in the U.S. context. The first has to do with the separation of church and state. The second is the demise of Christendom.

Separation of church and state became a political reality in the Protestant Reformation. After Martin Luther nailed his 95 theses on the church door in Wittenburg, Germany, in 1517, the Protestant Reformation engendered a number of Protestant denominations that in the American context competed for members, authority, and influence. Bradley Longfield (2013, 95) writes that in "the 1830s the Presbyterian General Assembly rivaled the federal government for popular influence and esteem." What was political expedient in the nineteenth century, is today no longer relevant because major moral issues, such as abortion, divorce, and homosexuality, are now decided through legislation and court decisions without reference to biblical warrant. The separation of church and state that allowed for freedom of religious affiliation—no official church—now effectively mandates a state religion without a church.

Christendom arose in the fourth century when Emperor Constantine (272–337 AD) adopted Christianity as the official religion of the Roman Empire (after 313 AD). When Christianity became an official religion, many new converts came into the church for reasons not necessarily related to faith. The need to define what it meant to be a Christian thus became a high priority. The Nicene Creed (325–381 AD), Apostle Creed (340 AD), and the Bible itself (367 AD) all date from this period. The demise of Christendom in this generation has reignited the identity question that had previously been a settled issue for roughly fifteen hundred years.

While some argue that Christendom's demise was long overdue, its absence reverberates throughout the church and complicates any attempt to define the church and its mission in this time and place. Likewise, the collapse of the separation of church and state means that the three signs of the true church (right preaching, right administration of sacraments, and church discipline) can no longer be assured (PCUSA 1999, 3.18). While the cause of these changes can certainly be argued, the existence of these changes is clear.

Return to a Biblical Church

While there was no one biblical institution called the church, the primary example of a church in the New Testament is the house church served by bi-vocational clergy. The New Testament gives no examples of professional clergy. The Apostle Paul worked as a tentmaker (Acts 18:3), which served as an interesting double-entendre. Paul made tents during the day and worked at night as an evangelist building the tabernacle (tent) of God.

∞

Blessed Lord Jesus,

All glory and honor, power and dominion, truth and justice are yours because you have walked among us, called us to be a people, and promised to be our God (Exod 6:7; Lev 26:12; Jer 1:4). May we all always hear your voice (Jer 7:23).

Forgive us, Lord, for amplifying our own voice and covering our ears when you speak to us. May we all always listen to your words.

Thank you for the blessings of Christian friendship,

comfort of family, and the many tangible things that you have placed in our lives. May we always harken to your voice.

In the power of your Holy Spirit, draw us to yourself. Open our hearts, illumine our thoughts, and strengthen our hands in your service. Set our hair on fire for your church.

In Jesus' previous name, Amen.

∞

Questions

1. What was the Apostle Paul's favorite name for the church?
2. What was the Old Testament concept of the church? To what purpose?
3. What was the purpose of the doctrine of separation of church and state? Why is that doctrine currently problematic?
4. When was Christendom established? What was the chief challenge back then?

The Postmodern Challenge

> *Jesus said to him, I am the way, and the truth, and the life.*
> *No one comes to the Father except through me.*
> (John 14:6)

*I*f the slander of Marx, Freud, and Nietzsche posed no philosophical threat to the church, more recent challenges have questioned both biblical authority and the church's witness to it.

The cultural-historical argument put forward by Jack Rogers (2009, 33), a Presbyterian theologian at San Francisco Theological Seminary and published by the Westminster John Knox Press, was evocative: The church got it wrong about slavery, women, and divorce. Now it has gotten wrong about homosexuality. Roger's book was used to launch a successful nationwide campaign within the Presbyterian Church (USA) to ordain homosexuals and to support gay marriage.

Roger's book goes on to challenge orthodox biblical hermeneutics. Where an orthodox approach to biblical interpretation would consider the author's intent, other statements in scripture, and the reader interpretation (Vanhoozer 1998, 25) in the original languages, Rogers (2009, 61) advises to focus on the double-love command. What would a loving God want us to say or do? While the role of love in Christian witness is undeniable, God's self-revelation to Moses is more complete: "The LORD, the LORD, a God merciful and gracious, slow to anger, and abounding in steadfast love and faithfulness." (Exod 34:6) God is love, but he is not only love.

While one might criticize Rogers as unrepresentative, unbiblical, and unorthodox, his critique has split the Presbyterian Church (USA) and other denominations since then. The problem is that his critique is at least partially true, and Roger's argument is intuitive to any rebellious teenager. In our anti-intellectual milieu, who has the patience to hear out a complex, theological rebuttal?

The crisis of authority that led to the reformation began with the infusion of humanism into the church. Roger's anthropological argument reiterates a similar humanistic critique. It's the Bible and tradition once again, but this time the tradition taken is from culture, not church practice. The reformers broke away from the Catholic Church to emphasize the authority of scripture much like the breakaway denominations today.

The Role of Materialism

At the time of the Reformation (after 1517), few

people doubted the metaphysical reality of God, and most people could not read a Latin Bible. When Luther and others translated the Bible into the languages commonly understood, this was something new and intriguing because most people could not read even their own native languages. When Calvin introduced public education in Geneva, it was expressly so that they could read their own Bibles.

Today in our materialistic culture, most Western people are functionally literate. What is different is that the metaphysical reality of God is openly ridiculed in public schools, in the media, and among intellectuals. Furthermore, the deconstructionism promoted by cultural Marxists questions all forms of authority (e.g. Marcuse 1974, 36) and leaves people suspicious of all leaders and radically isolated (Nouwen 2010, 12). A replay of the crisis of authority from the reformation accordingly plays differently in this new cultural context because by definition materialism precludes the existence of God.

Loss of Christendom and
Church-State Separation

Returning to this problem of the loss of Christendom

and church-state separation, the new cultural context provides no shelter from secular intrusion for our kids. Even as the formational concern becomes more critical for adults, our children are growing up without the benefit of having seen things work differently than the view given them on television, in public schools, and everywhere else they turn. Every flavor of perversion is immediately available and poses a claim on a kid's devotion even as parents fight daily to maintain standards of living and decency.

In this context, cultural Christianity offers no bulwark against the evil and slander of our time. The good news is that Christ died for our sins so that we don't have to.

∞

Almighty and Loving God,

All praise and honor, power and dominion, truth and justice are yours because you sent Christ to die for our sins and raised him from the dead.

We confess that by ourselves, we are lost and broken, unable to contend with the spirits of our day. Cast out the spirits that afflict us, cleanse our hearts, and redeem us for you alone.

We give thanks for the newness of the morning sun, the work that you have given us, and the comfort of family and church. Cast out the spirits that afflict us, cleanse our hearts, and redeem us for you alone.

In the power of your Holy Spirit, draw us to yourself. Open our hearts, illumine our thoughts, and strengthen us in your service.

In Jesus' precious name, Amen.

∞

Questions
1. What is the fundamental challenge to the church today?
2. What components make up orthodox biblical interpretation?
3. What five attributes of himself did God reveal to Moses? Why are they important today?
4. What crisis of authority arose during the reformation? Why is it different today?
5. What is materialism and why do we care?

OLD TESTAMENT IMAGES

Synopsis

The Old Testament introduces us to God who takes words seriously. The story of Abram begins with a promise that resembles a coming-of-age narrative. In the Exodus, this narrative is repeated for the people of Israel who in adversity learn to trust and rely on God. For those who refuse to acknowledge God, we see a cycle of sin, enslavement, crying out to the Lord, and God's provision of a savior. The Old Testament then walks us through a variety of divine revelations, actions, and covenants that prepare us for the better covenant in Christ and the gift of the Holy Spirit.

Authors and Words

> *And God said, Let there be light,*
> *and there was light.*
>
> (Gen 1:3)

*I*f a crisis of authority—a replay of the Reformation— is the core problem facing the church today, then the Old Testament experience provides insight. Understanding scripture starts with taking words seriously—God created the heavens and the earth with words. God's rule over creation is underscored by his creation with words in that "Ancient treaties [such as the creation covenant] were characterized as the 'words' of the suzerain [that is, king of kings]." (Niehaus 2014, 209) This seems odd to us because we live in a world where spin-doctors, advertisers, and half-truths undermine our confidence in the spoken word.

Not incidentally, the root of the word authority is author—an originator or creator of something. The New Testament makes this point several times when it describes Jesus as the "author and finisher of our faith" (e.g. Heb 12:2, KJV). The Greek word in view—*archenon* (BDAG 1154)—can mean: "One who has a preeminent position, leader, ruler, prince" or "One who begins something" or "One who begins or originates."

A crisis of authority can be characterized as a conflict among competing authorities. In Christian circles, this crisis is narrowly discussed in the context of disputes over the authority of scripture but because scripture defines our image of God, the crisis runs deeper. The materialistic world view, by defining God away, simply treats scripture as a cultural artifact, not an authority, and treats Christianity as a private preference with no claim on the body politic.

Creation Language

Consider the third verse of Genesis cited above where we are introduced to a moral creation. The verse appears straightforward. That is, until you start to reflect on what is said.

The verse consists of three phrases: "And God said," "Let there be light," and "and there was light." In English, the first phase is simply an attribution that tells us who is talking. The second phase is an invitation. The third is a simple declaration. We are not told how the invitation morphs into a declaration.

The original Hebrew text is no help in understanding these three phases. Phases two and third state exactly the same thing: Be light and [there] be light.

The grammatical description in my text (BDB 3570) describes the second phase as an apocopated jussive (abbreviated command), but that is likely an inference taken from the Greek translation in the Septuagint that utilizes an imperative form. If it is a jussive, then why does not the text simply read: God commanded that light be created? It could easily but it does not.

The grammatical translation in English, as in Greek, expresses unusual politeness, as a parent might employ with a child and the subtext is ethical: What God says; God does. This point is underscored in verse four: "And God saw that the light was good." (Gen 1:4) This form is repeated over and over in the creation accounts, which suggests emphasis and draws attention to the importance of words in the text.

Words and Actions

What if we assume a promise, not an imperative, in translating the third verse in Genesis: Be light and [there will] be light? This thought experiment can help us tease out insights that deepen our understanding of the text, a kind of meditative exercise not unlike *lectio divina*

(Peterson 2006, 91). Grammatically, this is not a stretch but only an interpretation no different than that expressed in an imperative.

Robert Jenson (1973, 2) writes: "A promise poses a future in a very particular way: as a gift." Creation is clearly a gift for Adam and Eve, And, by inference, for us. Jenson (1973, 8) interprets the Gospel as promise and views it as the grammatical anthesis of law.

> Because I will do such and such, you may await such and such. The pattern is 'Because...,' therefore...,' the reverse of 'If..., then...' Here the future is opened independent of any prior condition...it grants a future free from the past.

Viewing creation as a promise rather than an invitation is an interesting thought experiment for two reasons. First, the hearer participates actively in the future event—a formative process—rather than remaining a passive observer of the past. Second, it permits us to observe the agent of formation, the Holy Spirit.

Other Promises

The biblical template for faith in an individual is a coming-of-age story that begins when Abraham acts on God's promise (Gen 12:1–3). The biblical template for faith in a community begins with a promise to Moses:

Deliverance, freedom, and land (Exod 3:7–10). Formation occurs in accepting and sticking with the journey under guidance of the Holy Spirit.

Parenthetically, looking for places in the Old Testament where the Holy Spirit was active differs from the usual approach of noting where the text references the Holy Spirit. Jeffrey Niehaus (2014, 70-73) observes that the Holy Spirit is normally seen in the Old Testament as coming on or filling someone for a task or for a season, not inhabiting a person indefinitely as in the New Testament understanding. He gives the example: "Then Samuel took the horn of oil and anointed him in the midst of his brothers. And the Spirit of the LORD rushed upon David from that day forward." (1 Sam 16:13)

The Bible takes words seriously, yet the God of the Bible does not prefer any particular human language. The church could be defined as a community where people listen both to God and to one another.

∞

Almighty God, Author of Creation, Holy Spirit,

All praise and honor, power and dominion, truth and justice are yours because you have used words to create the universe and taught them to us.

Old Testament Images – 79

Forgive us when we persist in passivity, preferring darkness to light, and neglect to learn the words of our salvation.

Thank you for the witness of the saints, the gift of holy scripture, and the promise of a bright future with you.

In the power of your Holy Spirit, create in us a clean heart, O God, and renew a right spirit within us. Cast us not away from your presence, and take not your Holy Spirit from us. Restore to us the joy of your salvation, and uphold us with a willing spirit. (Ps 51:10–12)

In Jesus' precious name, Amen.

∞

Questions
1. Why should we treat words seriously?
2. What is the root of the word authority? Why do we care?
3. What happens if the imperative of Genesis 1:3 is interpreted instead as a promise?
4. What were God's promises to Abraham and Moses? Why do we care?
5. How do you define the current crisis of authority?

God's Promise to Abram

Now the LORD said to Abram,

Go from your country and your kindred

and your father's house

to the land that I will show you.

(Gen 12:1)

God's promise to Abram starts with a command—*Lek Leka*—which the King James version translates as "Get thee out." The modern translation of "Go" neglects the social context and spirit of the text. For those of modest means, a familiar social image emerges: A kid comes of age and gets kicked out of the house. The text leads us to believe that Abram is encouraged, not kicked, to leave the comfort and security of home with a series of inducements:

> And I will make of you a great nation, and I will bless you and make your name great, so that you will be a blessing. I will bless those who bless you, and him who dishonors you I will curse, and in you all the families of the earth shall be blessed. (Gen 12:2–3)

Because Abram was already seventy-five years old at this point (Gen 12:4), we do not normally think of this as a coming-of-age story. However, because his father Terah died at age two-hundred and five (Gen 11:32), compared with his father, Abram is not yet middle age.

Ruminations

A coming-of-age context here is important because Abram must learn to lead his family in a stressful time and unfamiliar place. His father, Terah, sets out to leave "Ur of the Chaldeans to go into the land of Canaan" (Gen 11:31) with son, Abram, and grandson, Lot, (and their wives) after Abram's brother Haran died in Ur. When they traveled to Haran, presumably Haran's home, Terah also died.

We are not told how or why the two men in the family died—Was it war, disease, famine?—but we can surmise that Abram's role as leader of the family is both sudden and mixed with tragedy. No one in their right mind in the ancient world would abandon the securities of family, tribe, and country without a strong inducement. Did God approach Abram as he struggled within a context of loss and anxiety? We are not told, but if Abram were leading a refugee family out of a war-torn land, then the social context here would make more sense, much like the kid kicked out of the house. One way or another, Abram's heart is open to the Holy Spirit's leanings and he goes.

Destination More Than a Place

If we try to intuit the role of the Holy Spirit in Abram's life, two conditions need to be met. First, the Holy Spirit needs to be an active agent, like the Apostle John's vision of the Paraclete (John 14:26). Second, Abram's life needs to be challenging, if a helper is to be any use.

What we see in the Genesis account is that Abram's life is full of challenges. Abram's story begins with the command to go to Canaan (Gen 12:1). The seventeen-hundred-mile journey from Ur of the Chaldeans to Jerusalem by foot would take around three months. Once he arrives, he finds the land inhabited by Canaanites. Abram builds alters at Shechem and Bethel, and, then, on account of a famine, he departs for Egypt (Gen 12:5–10).

What we see is a long journey marred by outward and inward obstacles. Outwardly, Abram cannot take possession of the Promised Land because it is already occupied by previous tenants. Inwardly, Abram's wife, Sarai, is barren, which the text discloses even as she introduced (Gen 11:30)—how can Abram's children increase to become a great nation? Circumstances need to change and Abram's faith needs to grow, if God's blessing is to come within reach. This is why it is helpful to interpret Abram's story as a coming-of-age narrative mentored by the Holy Spirit.

∞

Almighty Father,

All praise and honor, power and dominion, truth and justice are yours because you walk with us through the wilderness, shield us from harm, and mentor us when life's challenges seem overwhelming. Do not leave us to our own devices.

We confess that we are not always paying attention, heeding your promptings, or listening to your advice. Do not leave us to our own devices.

Thank you for the gift of scripture, the calming presence of your Holy Spirit, and the guidance of spiritual companions.

In the power of your Holy Spirit, open our hearts, illumine our thoughts, and strengthen our hands in your service.

In the precious name of Jesus, Amen.

∞

Questions
1. Why do we care about the translation of the command in Genesis 12:1?

2. What were the circumstances of Abram's departure from Haran?
3. How old is Abram when God commands him to leave Haran?
4. Why is it helpful to interpret Abram's story as a coming-of-age narrative?

Exodus, Wandering, and Entry

> *Then he said, Your name shall no longer be called Jacob,*
> *but Israel, for you have striven with God and with men,*
> *and have prevailed.*
>
> (Gen 32:28)

*T*he story of Abram serves as an introduction to the story of Moses, who is the author of both. Due to its length, we can intuit that Abram's story and those that followed had special meaning for Moses.

As the people of Israel left Egypt, they traveled to a land already promised to their ancestors, starting with Abram. But it was more than just land. Abram overcame many obstacles by obeying God's command. Likewise, the story of Joseph, Abram's great-grandson, served to explain why the people of Israel had become slaves in Egypt (Gen 37) and why their slavery was illegitimate (Exod 1:8). The stories in Genesis and Exodus are not randomly conceived, but served to offer hope that the current generation would face and overcome many obstacles.

The story of Moses begins with an enigmatic tale about recalcitrant midwives. Today we might describe their action as being faithful to the nudge of the Holy Spirit because they feared God more than the wrath of

Pharaoh (Exod 1:17). God rewarded their faithfulness: "And because the midwives feared God, he gave them families." (Exod 1:21) The text implies that they may have previously been barren or, at least, unable to children.

Faithful Midwives

The recalcitrance of the midwives serves as a bridge between the stories of Abram and Moses. Pharaoh's attempt to kill Hebrew boys stood as an impediment to God's promise to Abram that "I will make of you a great nation." (Gen 12:2) Once the nation of Israel has grown in Egypt from an extended family into a nation, the story of Moses transports them to the Promised Land to accomplish God's promise to Abram who now is truly Abraham, "The father of a multitude of nations." (Gen 17:5)

Moses' Call

Moses' journey of faith did not have a promising start. He was abandoned by his mother on the Nile in a basket, adopted by Pharaoh's daughter, and raised as a prince of Egypt (Exod 2:3–10). The first thing we learn about Moses as a young man is that he murdered an Egyptian and had to flee for his life to the deserts of Midian, where he lived the life of a shepherd (Exod 2:12–16). It was from the desert that God called Moses from the burning bush (Exod 3).

Consider God's instructions to Moses: "Come, I will send you to Pharaoh that you may bring my people, the children of Israel, out of Egypt." (Exod 3:10) It would not be easy to return to Egypt, having murdered an Egyptian and being already known within the household of Pharaoh. Imagine a convict returning to his hometown as a pastor, having been sent to prison for murder. Moses was not a credible witness among the Egyptians or his fellow Hebrews.

Transition From Slave To Free

Israel's departure from Egypt, sojourn in the desert, and entry into the Promised Land marked an important transition of faith. It may have taken forty days for Moses to lead the people of Israel out of Egypt, but it took forty years to get the Egypt out of the people (Bridges 2003, 43).

This three-way transition of faith is defined as a change broken up into the three emotional phases required. By contrast, a change simply describes the difference between an old state and a new one.

In the first phase, change is forced on you, but your

attention focuses on the things given up. In this first phase, the people of Israel say to Moses: "Is it because there are no graves in Egypt that you have taken us away to die in the wilderness?" (Exod 14:11) Then, they complained about food: "We remember the fish we ate in Egypt that cost nothing, the cucumbers, the melons, the leeks, the onions, and the garlic." (Num 11:5)

The second phase is the desert experience where one learns to depend on God (or not). Uncertainty and division mark this phase, but it was also a time of great opportunity for those who kept their heads in the midst of chaos. Consider the response of ten out of twelve of the spies sent into the Promised Land: "And there we saw the Nephilim (the sons of Anak, who come from the Nephilim), and we seemed to ourselves like grasshoppers, and so we seemed to them." (Num 13:33) For their lack of faith, God cursed the unfaithful among Israel to return to and die in the desert over the next forty years (Num 14:26–33). Only Joshua and Caleb, who returned with a faithful report and were willing to rely on God, would enter the Promised Land (Num 14:6–9).

The final phase arises once plans are set, and the

light at the end of the tunnel comes into view. In Joshua, we read:

> After the death of Moses the servant of the LORD, the LORD said to Joshua the son of Nun, Moses' assistant, Moses my servant is dead. Now therefore arise, go over this Jordan, you and all this people, into the land that I am giving to them, to the people of Israel. (Josh 1:1–2)

For the people of Israel to possess the Promised Land, they must take it from the current residents. Joshua, who had been Moses' right-hand man and leader of the military, was the ideal one to lead this effort (Exod 17:9).

Following the desert experience, the people of Israel were tough enough to pursue the path that God laid before them. The three-way transition—exodus, wandering, and entry—is not unlike a hospital visit—affliction, treatment, and recovery— or a college education—application, classes, and graduation. In each case, the middle of the transition is the hardest and, frequently, the most rewarding.

∞

Almighty Father,

All praise and honor, power and dominion, truth and justice are yours because you remain with us during our painful transitions sheltering us from harm when we are most vulnerable.

Forgive us when we are not our best selves, letting others down and not living into our faith.

Thank you for your divine presence, faithful guidance, and protection when other friends fail us and we find ourselves in confusing times.

In the power of your Holy Spirit, help us to lean away from our sinful, natural selves and into our new, faithful selves, and to listen to your faithful nudges. May we always find ourselves among your faithful remnant.

In Jesus' precious name, Amen.

∞

Questions
1. What lessons did Moses draw from the stories of Abram and his descendants?
2. What is interesting about the midwives of Egypt?
3. What is the role of the desert in Moses' call and Israel's formation?
4. What is the difference between a change and a transition?

The Deteronomic Cycle

We love because he first loved us.

(1 John 4:19)

While the stories of Abraham and of the Exodus offer positive responses of faith of at least a remnant, the Deuteronomic cycle given by Moses (Deut 30:1–3) and cited by Brueggemann (2016, 59) offers an alternative response. Those who refuse faith garner the curse of scattering, an echo of the curse of Cain (Gen 3:14). Here the pattern is collective sin, scattering and enslavement, crying out to the Lord, and the sending of a deliverer. This pattern is repeated throughout the Old and New Testaments. All are called; not all respond. One way or the other, through the instrumentality of the Holy Spirit, "To me every knee shall bow, every tongue shall swear allegiance." (Isa 45:23)

Cycle in Judges

The Deuteronomic cycle is especially prominent in the Book of Judges. The story of Gideon is a familiar example. The cycle starts with sin and the resulting curse. In Judges 6:1 we read: "The people of Israel did what was evil in the sight of the LORD, and the LORD gave them into the hand of Midian seven years." (Jdg 6:1) After being persecuted by the Midianites, the people cry out to the Lord in verse 6 and the Lord sends an angel to call on Gideon, who is busy hiding wheat from the Midianites in a winepress (verse 11).

Gideon then assembles three hundred men to fight an army of the Midianites described as locusts ravaging the land—too numerous to number. Responding to a vision in a dream, this team woke the Midianites in the middle of the night with trumpets and torches. Frightened in the night, the Midianites began slaughtering each other in the dark (Jdg 7:22). In this manner, the Lord freed the Israelite people from the oppression of the Midianites.

Cycle in Psalms

The Deuteronomic cycle usually applies to the people of Israel as a whole and brought salvation from oppression. However, following the pattern established in Psalm 18, Psalm 116 applies salvation to the individual rather than the nation. The cycle can once again be summarized as committing sin, earning the curse, crying out to the Lord, and then being redeemed.

The first four verses of Psalm 116 tell his story:

I love the LORD, because he has heard my voice and my pleas for mercy. Because he inclined his ear to me, therefore I will call on him as long as

I live. The snares of death encompassed me; the pangs of Sheol laid hold on me; I suffered distress and anguish. Then I called on the name of the LORD: O LORD, I pray, deliver my soul!

Verse one here explains his joy: "I love the LORD, because he has heard my voice and my pleas for mercy." Actually, English translations add the word, LORD, which does not appear in the original Hebrew or in the Septuagint Greek. The Hebrew simply reads: "I have loved because he has heard my voice." We see an echo of the original Hebrew in John's first letter: "We love because he first loved us." (1 John 4:19)

Moving on to verse two, the psalmist reiterates the importance of being heard and takes a vow: "Because he inclined his ear to me, therefore I will call on him as long as I live." This vow is interesting because if you pray or sing this psalm, as is the custom, you also repeat this vow.

Why is listening so important to the psalmist? Verse three reiterates the answer three times: "The snares of death encompassed me; the pangs of Sheol laid hold on me; I suffered distress and anguish." In other words, death had surrounded me; hell had opened its doors to pull me in; and I was terrified. The repetition assures us that the psalmist's vows in verse two are not to be taken lightly.

Verse four then closes the loop by returning to the second half of verse one. Verse one talks of pleas for mercy, while verse four cites the psalmist's actual prayer: "O LORD, I pray, deliver my soul!" Note that we are never told what sin the psalmist committed that precipitated these events—the sin is inferred, not stated.

What brings joy to the psalmist? The Lord rescued him from death. Commentators believe Psalm 116 to be a crib notes version of Psalm 18 where King David recounts his own brush with death (2 Sam 22).

New Testament Cycle

Psalm 116's personalized the Deuteronomic cycle and anticipated our salvation in Christ. In fact, if Jesus and the disciples sang Psalm 116 after the Last Supper, as was the custom during Passover, they took these very same vows and, in the resurrection, Jesus experienced God's deliverance.

The key to understanding this parallel is to see sin as a form of oppression. We all experience besetting sins—addictions small and great—that we cannot shake on our own. If gluttony is one of the seven deadly sins, it is also a besetting sin that can destroy our self-esteem, ruin our health, and undermine our relationships. Just like the Midianites oppressed Israel, we can be oppressed by besetting sins, and we need to cry out to the Lord for our forgiveness and salvation.

∞

Almighty God,

All praise and honor, power and dominion, truth and justice are yours because in your law you bless and curse us as we deserve, but in your Gospel through Jesus Christ you offer a path for redemption.

We confess that we are tempted to sin, to trespass against your law, and to commit all manner of iniquity. Forgive us. Help us to do better.

We give thanks for the many blessings of this life: Our creation, our families, our health, and useful work to do. Most of all, we give thanks for our salvation in Jesus Christ.

In the power of your Holy Spirit, draw us to yourself. Open our hearts, illumine our minds, strengthen our hands in your service.

In Jesus' name, Amen.

∞

Questions
1. Describe the components of the Deuteronomic cycle.

2. Give an example of how the Deuteronomic cycle appears in the Bible.
3. What are the implications of the Deuteronomic cycle for the idea of progress?
4. What happens if you pray or sing Psalm 116?

Scoring Covenants

> *I am the LORD your God,*
> *who brought you out of the land of Egypt,*
> *out of the house of slavery.*
> (Exod 20:2)

*I*f the Holy Spirit can be best found working in our lives in the midst of a painful journey, then the many divine symbols and experiences in the Old Testament can be scored by how well they drew the people in and pointed them to God. Given these criteria, the several Old Testament covenants stand out as especially important instruments of the Holy Spirit in the historical experience of Israel.

Weakness of Miracles, Signs, and Symbols

Miracles[1], signs, and symbols require interpretation. Much like a Rorschach test, the nature of the interpretation offered is often more a reflection of presuppositions of the observer than the intent of the author or creator.

The Prophet Hosea (8:4) wrote: "They made kings, but not through me. They set up princes, but I knew it not. With their silver and gold they made idols for their own destruction."

---

[1] C.S. Lewis (1974, 5) defines the word, miracle as "to mean interference with nature by supernatural power."

During my time as a hospital chaplain, I observed that the majority of people admitted to the emergency department suffered from preventable problems arising from poor lifestyle choices. If self-destruction is a theme in physical health, then how much more difficult is it to maintain good spiritual health? For such reasons, many of the Old Testament religious symbols had the potential to serve either to point to God or to become idols of fallen worship, like the fiery serpent fashioned by Moses (1 Kgs 18:4)[2]

In the New Testament, Jesus himself experienced a Gethsemane moment just before his arrest: Knowing that he would be arrested and sent to the cross, will he turn to God accepting his fate or run away to save his own life? (Matt 26:39) Our daily responses to pain—turning to God or into the pain—form who we are, much like the Prophet Job's relationship was strengthened by his experience of pain (Job 1:21). This is a opening for the Holy Spirit to form us, but the symbol or the pain is itself inherently ambiguous.

---

[2] Schlossberg (1990, 6) defines idolatry as "Any substitute of what is created for the creator."

Covenants Reliably Point to God

While many miracles, signs, and symbols are inherently ambiguous, divine covenants invite one into a long-term relationship with God.

The covenant provides objective boundaries and incentives to the relationship. Because of the long-term nature of the covenantal relationship, the covenant allows the Holy Spirit ample opportunities to shape the faith of participants. While the New Covenant in Christ is qualitatively better than prior covenants (Jer 31:33), the formative nature of the special grace covenants is already present in the covenants with Moses and David (Niehaus 2014, 32).

Niehaus (2014, 37) outlines the form of a Hittite covenant:

> [A] covenant is an expression of God's nature as a great suzerain who provides good things for his vassals, who imparts standards for their way of life, who will bless them for obedience and curse them for disobedience, and who is the eternal witness to these facts.

Covenantal stipulations provide for both blessings and curses, as articulated in Deuteronomy 28 for the Mosaic covenant, much like an employment contract (Niehaus

2014, 36).

Allied nations today have similar constitutional governance structures, trading treaties, and may offer space for military bases and ports of call to the superpower. Travel between the superpower and other nations in its domain is relatively easy so long as visitors abide by laws and bureaucratic conventions. The chief difference between today's treaties and a Hittite treaty is that a Hittite treaty is more inclusive of religious and lifestyle stipulations.

The New Covenant in Christ

The Prophet Jeremiah anticipated the limitations of the Old Testament covenants in pointing people to God:

> Behold, the days are coming, declares the LORD, when I will make a new covenant with the house of Israel and the house of Judah, not like the covenant that I made with their fathers on the day when I took them by the hand to bring them out of the land of Egypt, my covenant that they broke, though I was their husband, declares the LORD. For this is the covenant that I will make with the house of Israel after those days, declares the LORD: I will put my law within them, and I will write it on their hearts. And I will be their God, and they shall be my people. (Jer. 31:31-33)

Jeremiah describes covenantal law in paternalistic language ("I took them by the hand") that the people could not abide ("broke"). In other words, you can lead a horse to water, but you cannot make it drink.

The formational problem articulated by Jeremiah is not unlike the older brother's hardened heart in Jesus' Parable of the Two Brothers (or Prodigal Son), which is a New Testament coming of age story. The story begins with a father of two sons, neither of whom loves his father. The younger son demands his inheritance, runs off, and squanders it. When he falls into destitution, he remembers his father, and returns home to beg his father to offer him a job. When his father forgives him, the older son is angry, resentful, and even more bitter towards his father. The irony of this parable is that the younger and initially more outrageous son is the one who learns to love his father, a point that his older brother never reaches (Luke 15:11–31).

The qualitative superiority of the New Testament covenant in Christ arises, not because of our moral superiority to our ancestors or our greater intelligence with the advent of science, but because it permits the Holy Spirit greater opportunity to form and inform our faith in God.

∞

Almighty Father,

All praise and honor, power and dominion, truth

and justice are yours, because you nurtured our faith through covenants with Abraham, Moses, and David. While we broke covenant with you living in sin, you sent Christ to atone for that sin (Rom 5:8).

Forgive our hardened hearts, stopped up ears, and eyes blind to your many blessings.

Thank you for each and every new day.

In the power of your Holy Spirit, open our hearts, illumine our thoughts, and strengthen our hands in your service.

In Jesus' precious name, Amen.

∞

Questions
1. Why are miracles, signs, and symbols insufficient to engender faith?
2. What is the measure of a divine symbol?
3. What can we learn from self-destructive medical issues?
4. How is the new covenant in Christ qualitatively better than previous covenants?

THE HOLY SPIRIT IN LUKE - ACTS

Synopsis

The presence of the Holy Spirit is obvious in Luke's Gospel and the Book of Acts both from the number of citations and from the wandering ministry, healings, and wide interpretation of law that leaves room for guidance of the Holy Spirit. The call of the church is to minister to the world adopting the footloose characteristic of the Holy Spirit that stands in opposition to the exclusivity of the temple. Meanwhile, Luke presents at least three archetypal images of the church—the formal church, the communal church, and the house church. Each must balance out the congregational role of the church with its mentoring role to individuals.

Introduction to Acts

> *It seemed good to me also,*
> *having followed all things closely for some time past,*
> *to write an orderly account for you,*
> *most excellent Theophilus.*
>
> (Luke 1:3)

*T*he history of the early church is chronicled most extensively by Luke, who was Greek, a physician by trade, and a companion of Paul (Col 4:14). Luke was not among the original twelve disciples and wrote like a modern journalist. Modern scholars believe that Mark's Gospel is the oldest and that Luke's Gospel draws heavily on Mark as a source along with his own interviews. This makes sense because Luke was well acquainted with Mark, who served as *amanuensis* (scribe or secretary) of the Apostle Peter and is later believed to have traveled with Luke and Paul telling the Jesus story (2 Tim 4:11). Luke is also believed to have spoken extensively with Jesus' mother, Mary.

Luke's many references to the Holy Spirit set his Gospel apart. Luke mentioned the Holy Spirit more than twice as often as any other Gospel[1] writer and the Book of

---

[1] Matt 1:18, 20, 3:11, 12:32, 28:19; Mark 1:8, 3:29, 12:36, 13:11; Luke 1:15, 35, 41, 67, 2:25, 26, 3:16, 22, 4:1, 10:21, 11:13, 12:10, 12; John 1:33, 14:26, 20:22

Acts cited the Holy Spirit even more often[2]. A key passage in Luke is one of the first:

> And Mary said to the angel, How will this be, since I am a virgin? And the angel answered her, The Holy Spirit will come upon you, and the power of the Most High will overshadow you; therefore the child to be born will be called holy—the Son of God. (Luke 1:34–35)

If Jesus' conception is of the Holy Spirit, then everything that follows is too (Matt 1:18).

Luke's writing pays special attention to the role of women in Jesus' ministry, entourage, and financial support (Luke 8:3, Sproul 2005, 14). Only in Luke do we hear about Elizabeth, Mary's cousin, and the mother of John the Baptist (Luke 1) or Anna the Prophetess (Luke 2:36–37). Who, other than Mother Mary herself, could tell the story of her conversation with an angel? (Luke 1)

The Gospel of Luke serves as a prologue to the Book of Acts that focuses on the person of Jesus. Jesus' wandering ministry starts with temptations in the desert (Luke 4:1–13) that resemble the temptations of the people of the Israel during their sojourn in the wilderness (Wright 2004, 43). At least three aspects of Jesus' ministry highlight

[2] Acts 1:2, 5, 8, 16, 2:4, 33, 38, 4:8, 25, 31, 5:3, 32, 6:5, 7:51, 55, 8:15, 17, 19, 9:17, 31, 10:38, 44, 45, 47, 11:15, 16, 24, 13:2, 4, 9, 52, 15:8, 28, 16:6, 19:2, 6, 20:23, 28, 21:11, 28:25

the role of the Holy Spirit: The wandering ministry, Jesus' healings and exorcisms, and Jesus' interpretation of law.

Wandering Ministry

Jesus' traveling ministry parallels the wandering of Abram and the later wandering of the people of Israel during their time in the wilderness. For Abram and the people of Israel, this wandering is formative, and it teaches them to rely on God. For Jesus' disciples, the traveling ministry performs the same formative function, providing room in their lives for the work of the Holy Spirit.

Luke, whose purpose in writing is more analytical than the other Gospel writers, may actually have understood this point. Darrell Bock (1996, 146) observes:

> The unit in Luke divides clearly: An introduction (4:31–32), an exorcism (4:33–37), the healing of Simon's mother-in-law (4:38-39), another encounter with a demon (4:40–41), and a closing mission statement (4:42–44). Three miracle accounts dominate this description of Jesus' activity…. Mark tends to focus on the miracles themselves, while Luke balances his portrait between teaching, exorcism, and healing. For Luke words and deeds belong together.

If head and heart must be united in forming and informing our faith, then time is required to unite ideas with actions. Walking around and observing a teacher in action is not only an effective teaching method, it permits the Holy Spirit to work in one's heart and mind.

Jesus' wandering ministry, like mission trips today, likely benefitted the disciples' faith as least as much as those served.

Healings and Exorcisms

Jesus was the first medical missionary. More than that, his miraculous healings and exorcisms credentialed his claim to be the son of God because they point beyond the natural world to supernatural power (Lewis 1974, 5). Luke attributed such events to the Holy Spirit, such as when Jesus was baptized or led into the wilderness to be tempted (Luke 3:22, 4:1), more often than other Gospel writers.

Interpretation of Law

Jesus' interpretation of Jewish law offered room for the Holy Spirit to work in a person's life, which distinguished him from other teachers.

First, Jesus frequently posed an ethical dilemma, which places two legal principles in opposition to one another, to highlight his interpretation of law. He asked: "Is it lawful on the Sabbath to do good or to do harm, to save life or to destroy it?" (Luke 6:9) When the Pharisees refused to answer, Jesus healed a man with a withered hand and infuriated the Pharisees because the act of healing set a righteous act in opposition to their rules about work on the Sabbath (Luke 6:10–11).

This act of legal interpretation and healing embarrassed the Pharisees and put Jesus' life at risk, which lead him to a night of prayer and the calling of his disciples (Luke 6:12–16). Ironically, the healing could not be construed as work under the Sabbath laws because Jesus never touched the man (Wright 2004, 28).

Second, Jesus widened the interpretation of legal sanctions for murder, adultery, and other sins to consider the motivation behind the sin drawing attention to anger, lust, and other dark motives (e.g. Matt 5:20–22). This made compliance with the law impossible without divine intervention.

Technical compliance, as taught by the Pharisees, was not enough to assure righteousness. While Matthew's account of the Sermon on the Mount proscribes technical compliance, Luke's account promotes using rights under the law, such as enemy love and to witness to sinners (e.g.

Luke 6:27).

Using law to open disciples up to the Holy Spirit's intervention set Jesus' teaching apart from that of the Pharisees, who promoted strict adherence to precedent and a narrow definition of law. Those that have no sin feel no need of a savior. This is a problem today when people believe that they are basically good, which implies that they technically comply with law.

∞

Blessed Lord Jesus,

All praise and honor, power and dominion, truth and justice are yours because when we sought retribution, you taught us restoration, and when we wanted to pick nits, you gave eyes that see and ears that hear.

Forgive our narrow minds and shallow hearts. Help us to confess sins that we hide even from ourselves.

Thank you for the gift of the Holy Spirit, the spirit of truth and grace, the spirit of a new day and fresh thinking.

In the power of your Holy Spirit, open our hearts, illumine our thoughts, and strength our hands in your service.

In the name of the Father, the Son, and the Holy Spirit, Amen.

∞

Questions

1. What makes Luke an interesting Gospel writer? What sets him apart from the others?
2. Who is your favorite woman in the Gospel of Luke?
3. What three aspects of Jesus' ministry offer an opening to the Holy Spirit?
4. What sets Jesus' legal interpretation apart from the Pharisees?

The Call of the Church

But you will receive power
when the Holy Spirit has come upon you,
and you will be my witnesses in Jerusalem
and in all Judea and Samaria,
and to the end of the earth.

(Acts 1:8)

The Bible is a missionary document written by missionaries (Schnabel 2004, 5-6). The footloose character of the Holy Spirit as articulated in the Book of Acts must therefore be a controlling view throughout scripture. We see this already in the story of Abram where we, as stand-ins for Abram, are blessed to be a blessing (Gen 12:1–3). Rejecting this call to missions is effectively a rejection of our own election (McDonald 2010, 61, 97).

Rejecting the Call

Did the people of Israel lean into this idea of being a blessing to the nations around them?

The Prophet Jonah is instructive. God sends Jonah to preach to the Ninevites and he refuses; nevertheless, after being swallowed by whale, Jonah relents. He goes to Nineveh, prophesies their destruction, and the Ninevites turn to God (Schnabel 2004, 86–87). Jonah is neither surprised nor happy about this outcome (Jonah 4:1).

114 - *Image of the Holy Spirit and the Church*

This impulse to separate from other nations grew stronger during the Second Temple period following the Babylonian captivity:

> You see the trouble we are in, how Jerusalem lies in ruins with its gates burned. Come, let us build the wall of Jerusalem, that we may no longer suffer derision. (Neh 2:17)

When a nation is defined in terms of walled cities and faith in terms of temples, religion is more of a defense from foreign influences than an opportunity to be blessed and become a blessing to others. This is perhaps why no Shekinah cloud fills the rebuilt temple during this period.

This is the status of the people during the intra-testament period when there was no prophet in Israel after Malachi for four hundred years, which suggests why John the Baptist is often referred to as the last Old Testament prophet.

Crafting the Call

The core missionary intent is evident in Jesus calling his followers to be "fishers of people" and referred to them as "Apostles," which means: "envoys sent by the risen Jesus Christ to proclaim the good news" (Schnabel 2004, 10–12). Jesus describes his own mission when approached by Syrophoenician woman: "I was sent only to the lost sheep of the house of Israel." (Matt 15:24; Luke 4:43–44) Jesus saw himself as a missionary primarily to Israel, but the mandate for disciples to evangelize the world comes from the risen Christ just before his ascension: "You will be my witnesses in Jerusalem and in all Judea and Samaria, and to the end of the earth" (Acts 1:8; Schnabel 2004, 207).

This call to evangelize the nations is not restricted to Luke-Acts. Matthew also cites the Great Commission:

> Go therefore and make disciples of all nations, baptizing them in the name of the Father and of the Son and of the Holy Spirit, teaching them to observe all that I have commanded you. And behold, I am with you always, to the end of the age. (Matt 28:19-20)

The phrase—"I am with you always"—sounds suspiciously like a gift of the Holy Spirit. In John's Gospel, the parallel passage is "As the Father has sent me, even so I am sending you." (John 20:21) Mark's parallel passage is "Go into all the world and proclaim the gospel to the whole creation." (Mark 16:15)

When the calls to evangelize the world are cited, some will respond that these texts were late additions to the original manuscripts, but the texts themselves are full of efforts to train the disciples in evangelism. Consider Jesus' sending of his disciples ahead of his own traveling path, a kind of first-century advance-team:

> After this the Lord appointed seventy-two others and sent them on ahead of him, two by two, into every town and place where he himself was about to go. And he said to them, The harvest is plentiful, but the laborers are few. Therefore pray earnestly to the Lord of the harvest to send out laborers into his harvest. (Luke 10:1–2)

And what training had the disciples received in evangelism, other than to live with Jesus and know him? The disciples were given no resources and were instructed to live among the people: "Carry no moneybag, no knapsack, no sandals, and greet no one on the road." (Luke 10:4)

While the Holy Spirit had not yet been formally given to them, the disciples' report suggests that informally the Holy Spirit had already empowered them: "Lord, even the demons are subject to us in your name!" (Luke 10:17) By any line of thinking, exorcism is a ministry of power, a test of wills within a spiritual context.

The Greater Context

While seeds of this view of missions and the church's call are found throughout scripture, Luke is the one who develops this vision most clearly. Note that the church's mission statement (Acts 1:8) is given before the granting of the Holy Spirit at Pentecost (Acts 2:1–4).

∞

Almighty Father,

All praise and honor, power and dominion, truth and justice are yours because you have trained us to be aware of and minister to those around us.

Forgive us when we prefer to focus on ourselves and neglect to share the Gospel of Jesus that heals our souls, builds up our families, and nurtures a community of trust and faithfulness.

Thank you for the ministry of the saints, the person of Jesus, and the gift of the Holy Spirit.

In the power of your Holy Spirit, open our hearts, illumine our thoughts, and strengthen our hands in your service.

In Jesus' precious name, Amen.

∞

Questions
1. What is the mission of the church?
2. When was the Holy Spirit most obviously given? When else has the Holy Spirit been present?
3. What did Jesus say his mission was?
4. Name the calls to evangelize in each of the four Gospels.

The Footloose Holy Spirit

> *And it shall come to pass afterward,*
> *that I will pour out my Spirit on all flesh;*
> *your sons and your daughters shall prophesy,*
> *your old men shall dream dreams,*
> *and your young men shall see visions.*
> (Joel 2:28)

*T*he importance of the Holy Spirit in the Book of Acts is highlighted in the first sentence in the Greek where the Risen Christ is described as giving "Commands through the Holy Spirit to the apostles." (Acts 1:2) The Apostles will be "baptized with the Holy Spirit" (Acts 1:5), "receive power," and become "witnesses" (Acts 1:8).

On the Day of Pentecost with the founding of the church, the Apostle Peter cites the Prophet Joel anticipating the pouring out of the Holy Spirit on all flesh, including young men and women, old men, and even servants through prophesy, dreams, and visions (Joel 2:28). Significantly, one of the charges that Stephen laid before the High Priest and the Sanhedrin before he was stoned was that they (and their fathers) habitually resisted the Holy Spirit (Acts 7:51).

Resisting the Holy Spirit

From a strict first-century Jewish perspective, the

outpouring of the Holy Spirit at Pentecost displayed the footloose characteristic of the spirit because it came outside the bounds of established religion. This perception was nowhere more pronounced than in the person of Saul of Tarsus, who initially persecuted Christians in the name of God:

> "But Saul was ravaging the church, and entering house after house, he dragged off men and women and committed them to prison. Now those who were scattered went about preaching the word." (Acts 8:3–4)

Saul resisted the Holy Spirit, as Stephen had alleged, but could not help but be an agent of the Spirit's work because the word continued to be preached and in new places! Important first-century churches, such as in Antioch and Rome, were founded presumably by this diaspora of ordinary believers scattered by this persecution.

Taiwanese Pentecost

A modern example of an outpouring of the Holy Spirit occurred among indigenous mountain people in Taiwan, who Christian missionaries tried, but could not reach. Even the Japanese who controlled the coastal areas of Taiwan during their WWII occupation were unable to subjugate these mountain people, who maintained their independence and practiced headhunting as a rite of passage into manhood.

Ralph Covell (1998, 167) writes about how an ordinary woman, Chi Wang, from the Sedig people came to faith in a coastal area in the 1930s. She returned to the mountains on her own to spread a simple understanding of the Gospel. Her message incited a revival among these people during the occupation in spite of almost complete isolation from other Christians.

Today there is a church named for her that meets in a large cave where she used to hold meetings. Chi Wang, like many of the Sediq church leaders who followed, had little or no formal education (Covell 1998, 169–174). Chi Wang passed away in 1946.

If the Holy Spirit can bring salvation to headhunters in Taiwan, who is beyond the love of God?

Paul's Conversion

The reach of the Holy Spirit in the Book of Acts knows few bounds. The miraculous conversion of the Ethiopian Eunuch (Acts 8:26–40), the pouring out of the Holy Spirit on the household of Cornelius (Acts 10:44), and baptism of the Macedonian jailer and his family (Acts 16:33) all display the Holy Spirit's power and reach, as confirmed by the Jerusalem Council. (Acts 15:8). None of these events were as dramatic, however, as the conversion of Saul, persecutor of the church.

The Book of Acts reports Saul's conversion three times (Acts 9, 22, 26) to advance the goal: "But you will receive power when the Holy Spirit has come upon you, and you will be my witnesses in Jerusalem and in all Judea and Samaria, and to the end of the earth." (Acts 1:8) Later Saul preferred to be known by his Gentile name, Paul. Because Paul's career as an evangelist took him "to the ends of the earth," possibly Spain, but most assuredly Rome, Luke could write about the advance of the Great Commission to all nations (Matt 28:19) using Paul's apostolic biography and numerous speeches written in the first person to personalize his message.

The Hermeneutic Challenge

Parenthetically, talking about the agency of the Holy Spirit poses an interpretational problem, especially in our materialistic culture. For the Christian, it is easy to interpret actions and events displaying divine agency because Christians believe that the material world can illumine a spiritual reality—a form of lesser-to-greater argumentation. Thus, when John the Baptist asks Jesus: "Are you the one who is to come, or shall we look for another?" (Luke 7:20) Jesus responds:

> Go and tell John what you have seen and heard: the blind receive their sight, the lame walk, lepers are cleansed, and the deaf hear, the dead are raised up, the poor have good news preached to them. (Luke 7:22)

John would easily hear this statement as referencing Isaiah 61, a claim of Messianic commission obviously transcending the materialistic worldview. Others observing the same actions today might interpret them as a magic trick, a neat story, or medical expertise, consistent with their materialistic worldview.

∞

Almighty Father, Beloved Son, Spirit of Truth,

All praise and honor, power and dominion, truth and justice are yours because you reach us in our sin and grant us ears that hear and eyes that see.

Forgive us of our predilections, our prejudices, and unsavory thoughts, our evil actions and thankless hearts.

We give thanks for your Holy Spirit, who comes to us where we are and heals our hearts, minds, and blooded hands.

In the power of your Holy Spirit, grant us open hearts, discerning minds, and helping hands. Do not give us over to our wanton desires or the hands of grasping, evil people.

In Jesus' precious name, Amen.

∞

Questions

1. What are some signs of the Holy Spirit's presence among us?
2. What does it mean to resist the Holy Spirit?
3. What are signs of the Holy Spirit according to the Prophet Joel?
4. What is interesting about the history of the church in Taiwan?

Temple Abandonment

> Jesus *answered them, Destroy this temple,*
> and *in three days I will raise it up.*
> The *Jews then said, It has taken forty-six years*
> to *build this temple,*
> and *will you raise it up in three days?"*
> (John 2:19–20)

*T*he Holy Spirit is the presence of God among us. For the Jew, God's presence was associated with the Shekinah cloud presumably found in the Jerusalem Temple. This is why temple sacrifices were important—the sacrifices were presented directly to God. When Jesus spoke about destroying the Jerusalem Temple, the Jewish people would think about the Shekinah cloud and the sacrifices.

Religious and Economic Conflict

For the Sadducees (the high priestly class), it was a threat to their livelihood and the livelihood of the many people in and around Jerusalem who provided animals for sacrifice. It would be like threatening to shut down Wall Street in New York City or the casinos in Las Vegas. Some scholars have suggested that Jesus was crucified, not so much for claiming to be the Son of God, as for clearing the temple marketplace (e.g. Luke 19:45) and threatening to destroy the temple (e.g. John 2:19–20).

Yoder (1994, 60) would add that Jesus' life was treated because he advocated Jubilee, an important reference of which was found in Isaiah 61:2—the text referenced in Jesus' call sermon (Luke 4:19). Jubilee implied: "Four prescriptions: 1. Leaving the soil fallow; 2. The remission of debts; 3. The liberation of slaves, 4. The return of each individual of his family's property." Three out of the four prescriptions would sound highly contentious to the ruling class in Jerusalem. Think about the stir created in Washington when the President advocated forgiving (remitting) student loan debt.

Temple Abandonment

Temple abandonment is a phrase that implies that God is withdrawing his presence, a sort of divine curse or "dark night of the soul." King David spoke of this same concept when he wrote "Cast me not away from your presence, and take not your Holy Spirit from me." (Ps 51:11) David had witnessed first-hand how withdrawing God's presence from King Saul had left him a tormented individual, who eventually lost his kingship (e.g. 1 Sam 16:1).

In Luke's writing, temple abandonment is hinted at

many times, but two stand out: The tearing of the curtain in the temple during the crucifixion (Luke 23:45) and the stoning of Stephen (Acts 7:58) that was precipitated by the accusation that he repeated Jesus' statement about destroying the temple (Acts 6:14).

The tearing of the curtain in the temple opened access to God as when Jesus declared people's sins to be forgiven. Temple sacrifices (e.g. Lev 4:35) were no longer necessary for the forgiveness of sins, and the monopoly of temple priests to God's presence was broken. It is therefore fair to describe temple abandonment as being at the heart of the Gospel message.

Destruction of the temple was the ultimate threat to Jewish priests, not only because it put them out of a job, but because the Jewish faith required sacrifices that could no longer be made. The temple was also an enduring reminder of the Davidic kingdom—How could God's messiah restore the Jewish kingdom if its most important symbol were destroyed? Even Jesus' own disciples asked the Risen Christ: "Lord, will you at this time restore the kingdom to Israel?" (Acts 1:6)

Dark Night of the Soul

The phrase "dark night of the soul" is attributed to Saint John of the Cross (1542–1591), who was a Spanish mystic and Carmelite priest writing during the counter-reformation period. This dark night of the soul presumably arises when God cloaks his presence from us as a test to see if we truly love him, not just seek his blessings. Zimmerman writes: "The purpose of these trials is, however, not to throw the soul into despair but to wean it from all comfort so as to leave it with no other support than God himself." (Saint John, 2006, xxi). Therefore, God's withdrawal from the temple should be seen as a teaching moment, not total abandonment, much like the period of the wilderness pilgrimage (Num 14:26–35).

Your Body as God's Temple

Obviously, when the Apostle Paul wrote—"Your body is a temple of the Holy Spirit within you" (1 Cor 6:19)—his comment suggests that the Jerusalem temple was no longer the symbol of God's presence that it once was. If your body is designed to be a temple of the Holy Spirit, then failing to invite the Holy Spirit in is tantamount to inviting demonic possession—a practical result of temple abandonment (Niehaus 2014, 130–131).

The ultimate statement of temple abandonment arose in Jesus' prophecy on the Mount of Olives (Luke 19:41–44) that anticipated the destruction of Jerusalem and its temple by the Romans, which took place in AD 70. The temple was never rebuilt, which denied adherents to biblical Judaism the ability to perform required sacrifices. For Christians, Christ's death on cross became the final sacrifice for sin and the source of our salvation..

∞

Almighty Father,

All praise and honor, power and dominion, truth and justice are yours because you tabernacle with us, offering your presence, guidance, and strength.

Forgive our hardened hearts, closed minds, and grasping fingers. Lead us where you would want us to go.

Thank you for your everlasting spirit, the hope of our future with you, and every imageable blessing.

In the power of your Holy Spirit, teach us your ways, remind us of your word, and help us to be fully present to those around us.

In Jesus' precious name, Amen.

∞

Questions
1. How would you describe temple abandonment?
2. Why is Jubilee interesting?
3. How does forgiveness of sins relate to temple abandonment?
4. What is interesting about your body being a temple of the Holy Spirit?

Images of the Church

And Peter said to them, Repent
and be baptized every one of you
in the name of Jesus Christ
for the forgiveness of your sins,
and you will receive the gift of the Holy Spirit.
(Acts 2:38)

*T*he Book of Acts characterizes the church with at least three stylized images—the formal church, the communal church, and the household church—that overlap and remain laconic in Luke's narrative, but remain influential in the church today.

The Formal Church

The first image of the church in Acts focuses on the formalities of baptism and confirmation. Living into these formalities grants the believer forgiveness of sins and the gift of the Holy Spirit. Today baptism is frequently practiced on babies and, when they grow old enough, their faith is confirmed with a public declaration in front of the congregation. In other traditions, a profession of faith is made in anticipation of baptism consistent with the passage above in Acts 2:38. The Apostle Peter's sermon on Pentecost embraced these formalities—baptism and confirmation—that still define church membership today.

The Communal Church

The second image of the church focuses on the strength of commitment, especially as it pertains to helping others. Here we read:

> And all who believed were together and had all things in common. And they were selling their possessions and belongings and distributing the proceeds to all, as any had need. And day by day, attending the temple together and breaking bread in their homes, they received their food with glad and generous hearts, praising God and having favor with all the people. And the Lord added to their number day by day those who were being saved. (Acts 2:44–3:1)

The image here pictures the church as an extended family where family members are cared for according to their basic needs. Hellerman (2001, 2) attributes the rapid growth of the early church to its role as a surrogate family.

This growing relationship with Jesus is especially important in times and places, such as in missions, where persecution renders formal church membership dangerous.

House Churches

The third image of the church comes from the observation that family leaders often brought their entire households—many of whom were not blood relatives—

to be baptized together. In the Book of Acts this family conversion experience is explicit in the case of the family of Cornelius (Acts 10:44) and the Macedonian jailer (Acts 16:33), but we know from Paul's writing that many churches met in particular households, whose families could presumably share the space.

House churches are increasingly important today where full-time, paid ministry is impossible and formal church membership is illegal or the object of persecution. Bi-vocation pastors often cannot afford to buy or rent space for a church. In some mega churches, active small groups also function as de-facto house churches offering greater intimacy than is possible within the wider church community.

Archetypal Church Images

The archetypes of the early church given in the Book of Acts continue to influence how we think about and organize the church today. Formalities, like baptism and confirmation, play a bigger role in established denominations, like Presbyterians, Episcopalian, and Lutheran denominations, than in newer Pentecostal and Charismatic denominations, where house churches are almost the norm. Churches more focused on social ministry have a special relationship with the communal model of church.

The primacy of the formal church articulated by the Apostle Peter needs to be underscored, because that's where the blessings lie. The second and third images of the church (and all others) presume that the believer lives into the first image because efforts to deny or minimize the importance of the first image undermine the legitimacy of alternative church images, of which there are many. Missing from these three images are churches defined by cultural and ethnic affinities, facility attributes, location, programs, pastoral expertise, and staff size so often important today in building membership.

While such alternative images of the church can be criticized as distractions that undermine church legitimacy, God meets us where we are but does not leave us there. The Holy Spirit routinely uses imperfect people and churches to challenge our faith and draw us closer to himself, as the Book of Acts illustrates in the person of Saul of Tarsus.

Economics and Church Structure

The economic status of churches also influences their choice of church models as it affects their ability to support full-time, seminary-trained, paid staff. Perceptions of the church's status in society, the role of Christians in the culture, and the self-image of Christians are likewise influenced by their preferred church model.

How does a formal church adjust to becoming a house church after their pastor retires or has been laid off? It's like the college graduate who has been forced to move back home with mom and dad—the humiliation is likely to outweigh the economic advantage. Many such churches simply sell their property and close their doors; others band together (yoke) with another local church to hire a pastor; still others employ bi-vocational pastors. It is much easier for a house church to grow to become a formal church than vice versa.

Declining standards of living are a reality for many Christians today. As economic fortunes change and affect the organizational structure of churches, how do churches adjust to such changes while simultaneously encouraging their members to remain faithful? While it is clear that churches often function as social shock-absorbers for individuals who undergo difficult transitions, it is less clear that they manage change well at times when they themselves need to adapt and remain open to the nudge of the Holy Spirit.

∞

Merciful Father,

All praise and honor, power and dominion, truth and justice are yours because you come to us through the faithful witness of churches of all shapes and sizes.

Forgive us when we fail ourselves and others in our work and family life.

Thank you for the gift of fellowship, Christian community, and spiritual friends.

In the power of your Holy Spirit, draw us to yourself. Open our hearts, illumine our thoughts, and strengthen our hands in your service.

In Jesus' precious name, Amen.

∞

Questions
1. Name three types of churches mentioned in the Book of Acts.
2. How to these church types inform congregational life today?
3. What are three ways churches respond to declining fortunes?

Luke's Paraclete

> *But the Helper [the Paraclete], the Holy Spirit,*
> *whom the Father will send in my name,*
> *he will teach you all things and bring to your remembrance*
> *all that I have said to you.*
> (John 14:26)

*T*he *Paraclete* in John's Gospel is a messenger, teacher, and memory-jogger. The *Paraclete* serves as a divine mentor requested by Jesus himself and sent by the Father (John 14:16; 15:26). Luke does not mention the *Paraclete* in either his Gospel or the Book of Acts, but he introduces us to Joseph of Cyprus, whose mentoring played a critically important role in the early church.

Barnabas the Mentor

Joseph of Cyprus, a Levite, is better known to Christians as Barnabas, a nickname given him by the Apostles. In Hebrew, Barnabas means son of the prophet, but Luke tells us that it means son of encouragement, a metaphorical inference (Acts 4:36).

The nickname was likely given because Joseph made a substantial donation to the early church (Acts 4:37), which demonstrated encouragement because of timeliness and need. But the second time that Barnabas is mentioned his encouragement takes an entirely different turn:

> And when he [the Apostle Paul] had come to Jerusalem, he attempted to join the disciples. And they were all afraid of him, for they did not believe that he was a disciple. But Barnabas took him and brought him to the apostles and declared to them how on the road he had seen the Lord, who spoke to him, and how at Damascus he had preached boldly in the name of Jesus. (Acts 9:26–27)

Bringing Paul to the Apostles took moxy—Paul had previously been a persecutor "ravaging the church" (Acts 8:3) and, out of fear, the Apostles shunned him.

Mentoring Beyond Words

But Barnabas did not stop with introductions—he actively mentored him in ministry. When the Apostles heard that the Antioch Church was growing, they sent Barnabas to investigate. Barnabas worked with the Antioch Church and his ministry helped them grow. But Barnabas saw more potential:

> So Barnabas went to Tarsus to look for Saul, and when he had found him, he brought him to Antioch. For a whole year they met with the church and taught a great many people. And in Antioch the disciples were first called Christians. (Acts 11:25–26)

Antioch was one of the first century's most important churches, but this was also where—thanks to Barnabas—Paul learned to be an evangelist. This after previously having been effectively exiled by the Apostles to his hometown in Tarsus.

It was in Antioch that Paul received his Gentile commission:

> The Holy Spirit said, set apart for me Barnabas and Saul [Paul] for the work to which I have called them. Then after fasting and praying they laid their hands on them and sent them off." (Acts 13:2–3)

Note that the commission is attributed to the Holy Spirit and that Barnabas continued his work of mentoring Paul even during his first missionary trip.

Fruit of Mentoring?

Petty, self-serving, and weak leadership is more typical than good mentoring in most organizations, not just the church. Recently I learned of a pastoral colleague and friend who has been taken offline because from an accusation of just one individual. One-strike-you-are-out behavior is an all-too-typical employment practice in our competitive world that undermines institutional innovation as staff and managers grow more risk-averse.

The alternative is to teach and focus on mentoring. Paul Moots (2014, 2–3) writes:

> The ministry of encouragement is the art of leading and supporting others in the discovery of their own spiritual gifts and call to discipleship...We can become a Barnabas...encouragement allows the congregation to shape its ministry around its strengths rather than to base its work on some model derived from another congregation's story, another pastor's experience.

What if Barnabas had just tooted his own horn, ignored the Apostle Paul's talents and shunned him like everyone else?

Paul's evangelism established churches throughout Asia Minor into Greece all the way to Rome. He also personally wrote more than half the books of the New Testament (NT) and likely motivated authors to write most of the other NT books. These accomplishments helped form the foundation of the early church. None of them would have been done (or at least they would have been delayed) had Barnabas not mentored Paul. This is why it is fair to describe Barnabas as Luke's Paraclete.

∞

Gracious Father,

All praise and honor, power and dominion, truth

and justice are yours because at just the right time you sent Christ to die for our sins, sent evangelists into our world so that we might learn about it, and sent mentors into our lives that we might carry the word to others.

Forgive us our myopic vision, our grasping hands, and our empty hearts. Teach us to love the things that you love.

Thank you for the life and ministry of Barnabas. Help us to emulate his strength, vision, and willingness to serve.

In the power of your Holy Spirit, make us Paracletes to those around us.

In Jesus's name and for your glory, Amen.

∞

Questions
1. What does the name Barnabas mean?
2. What two types of encouragement did Barnabas offer?
3. Where was the title of Christian first used?
4. What was the fruit of Barnabas' mentoring?

THE CHURCH IN PAUL'S WRITING

Synopsis

The Apostle Paul mentored the churches that he founded in their spiritual walk through his letters and visits, and he viewed them as an extension of the people of Israel. This conclusion is obvious from Paul's use of Old Testament scripture and his view of the Holy Spirit as a spiritual mentor and grantor of spiritual gifts for ministry. Paul also promoted an egalitarian interpretation of relations within the family that he later used as a model for the church. Paul viewed the distinctiveness of the church as arising from its pursuit of holiness in an unholy cultural context. Mentoring thus played a special role in Paul's approach to developing church leaders, such as Timothy.

Visions of the Church

To all those in Rome who are loved by God
and called to be saints...
First, I thank my God through Jesus Christ for all of you,
because your faith is proclaimed in all the world.
(Rom 1:7–8)

*T*he Apostle Paul "writes pastoral letters to Christian communities, not evangelistic or apologetic treatises" (Hays 1989, 86). Paul's focus is on Christian formation. "Paul does not speak of ethics as such, but of how to walk, the primary term for ethical conduct" (Thompson 2011, 1, 61). This suggests that *telos* (Greek for an end or a future goal), not identity or duty, drives Pauline ethics, but it also directs our attention to the Holy Spirit. When one is on a journey, one elicits the services of a guide—no guide is needed to sit and passively observe.

The Journey

At the core of Christian faith is the observation that the universe was created at a point in time (Gen 1:1) and will one day come to an end (Niehaus 2017, 4). In Revelation, this point is made explicit: "Fear God and give him glory, because the hour of his judgment has come, and worship him who made heaven and earth, the sea and the springs of water." (Rev 14:7) The Christian faith starts and ends in historical time, not seasonal or mythical time.

In the church, we are collectively on a journey through time where formation matters and a guide is needed if things are to end well. The Apostle Paul is accordingly an instrument of the Holy Spirit in the general sense attributed to authors of canonical scripture and in the specific sense that he focuses on Christian formation. Paul's pastoral letters are straightforward mentoring of the churches that he helped establish.

This simple insight responds to a key problem facing postmodern people: A lost sense of history. Life being stuck in a moment implies no history, no duty, and no future—hence, no meaning. People anesthetize themselves with activities, media, drugs, pets, and so on. It's as if one were floating in space as an accidental speck of meaningless dust. Because everything depends on expending energy, exhaustion is a constant companion. Nothing changes, so our mistakes, our weakness, and our sins haunt us forever. Thanks be to God for our creation, our redemption, and our future in Christ.

Vision for the Church

Richard Hays (1989, 88-91) studied Paul's use of scripture in Second Corinthians 8:15 and reached an interesting conclusion. In Paul's discussion of raising money to support the Jerusalem church, he cites the wilderness experience: "Whoever gathered much had nothing left over, and whoever gathered little had no lack." (Exod 16:18)

While Paul uses this passage to argue for equality between the two churches, implicitly he compares the church's journey of faith to Israel's wilderness experience. By inference, he sees the church not so much replacing as continuing the people of Israel, which Paul makes explicit in his grafting analogy in Romans 11 (Hays 1989, 90, 96).

This makes perfect sense, if faith is primarily a relationship rather than a membership in any particular community. The formalities of faith, as suggested by the Apostle Peter's sermon on Pentecost (Acts 2:38), primarily serve to confirm the relationship. However, even in Paul's own writing, there is tension between faith as relationship and the formalities of faith (1 Cor 11:23–26).

The Church as a Grafted Branch

The continuity of the church with Israel is made most explicitly in Paul's analogy of the grafting of new believers onto an olive tree, his analogy for Israel:

> For if you were cut from what is by nature a wild olive tree, and grafted, contrary to nature, into a cultivated olive tree, how much more will these, the natural branches, be grafted back into their own olive tree. (Rom 11:24)

In grafting, one tree does not replace another because they become one tree. Hays (1989, 96–97) observes: "Paul never uses expressions such as the *new Israel* or *spiritual Israel*. There always has been only one Israel."

This discussion of olive trees may sound casual or incidental to modern readers, but for Jews this is a serious issue because it implies that the blessings bestowed on Israel continue in the church. This includes the mentorship of the Holy Spirit. The wilderness experience of Israel and the temple with the Shekinah cloud continue in the church.

∞

Almighty Father,

All praise and honor, power and dominion, truth and justice are yours because you guide us through the deserts of life to bring us closer to yourself and protect us amidst much strife (Ps 91:2–7).

Forgive us when we try to go it alone, ignoring your council and pretending that we are able to manage on our own (Num 20:7–12). Do not leave us at the mercy of our own desires.

Thank you for the many blessings given to Israel (Deut 28:2–14) and conveyed to the faithful of the church (Rom 11), especially the blessing of your presence.

In the power of the Holy Spirit, draw us to yourself. Open our hearts, illumine our thoughts, and strengthen our hands in your service.

In Jesus' precious name, Amen.

∞

Questions
1. Why is it important to recognize that Paul wrote pastoral letters to the church?
2. What is the nature of ethical conduct for Paul?
3. Why is history important for the Christian?
4. What is the analogy of the olive tree?
5. What are some examples of God's provision and presence?

The Holy Spirit and Scripture

But the word is very near you. It is in your mouth
and in your heart, so that you can do it.

(Deut 30:14)

*T*he Holy Spirit plays a crucial role in the Apostle Paul's reading of scripture because scripture can only be understood through the inspiration of the Holy Spirit. When the Corinthian church asked Paul for his letters of recommendation, he replied:

> You yourselves are our letter of recommendation, written on our hearts, to be known and read by all. And you show that you are a letter from Christ delivered by us, written not with ink but with the Spirit of the living God, not on tablets of stone but on tablets of human hearts. (2 Cor 3:2–3)

His letter of recommendation was the work of the Holy Spirit in the life of Corinthian church.

At this point, Paul turned to an enigmatic story of how Moses' face shone when he communed with God, so much that he had to veil his face:

> But their minds were hardened. For to this day, when they read the old covenant, that same veil remains unlifted, because only through Christ is it taken away. Yes, to this day whenever Moses is read a veil lies over their hearts. But when one turns to the Lord, the veil is removed. Now the

Lord is the Spirit, and where the Spirit of the Lord is, there is freedom. (2 Cor 3:14–17)

In this same way, when one reads scripture outside the context of faith, it remains veiled and can only be unveiled through the power of the Holy Spirit. In summarizing Paul's hermeneutical method, Hays (1989, 191) writes: "No reading of scripture can be legitimate if it fails to shape the readers into a community that embodies the love of God as shown forth in Christ."

This is why when Paul speaks of faith, he speaks in terms of this unveiling as when he writes, paraphrasing Deuteronomy 30:14:

> The word is near you, in your mouth and in your heart (that is, the word of faith that we proclaim); because, if you confess with your mouth that Jesus is Lord and believe in your heart that God raised him from the dead, you will be saved. For with the heart one believes and is justified, and with the mouth one confesses and is saved. For the Scripture says, Everyone who believes in him will not be put to shame. (Rom 10:8–11)

This unveiling metaphor is crucial to understanding both Paul's hermeneutical method and the mystery of faith: Both require the instrumentality of the Holy Spirit.

Implicit in Paul's copious use of Old Testament scripture is the continuity of the people of Israel with the church, a theme explicitly drawn out in Paul's grafting analogy in Romans 11. The curiosity of scriptural echoes arises in Paul's writing as a tension between theme and counter-theme. Hays (1989, 46) writes:

> In Romans 1:18–3:20, even where Paul uses scriptural allusions to underscore the message of God's judgment, the texts themselves whisper the counter-theme of God's mercy.

This statement jumps out at me because this passage is used by some commentators to hammer people, like a Bible-over-the-head, and is much reviled by others. Hays (1989, 47) refers to this as the "judgment/grace paradigm that undergirds the whole witness of Scripture."

The role of the Holy Spirit in Paul's hermeneutical method is so basic that it sometimes goes unnoticed. Consider the famous passage in Timothy:

> All Scripture is breathed out by God [*Theopneumatos*] and profitable for teaching, for reproof, for correction, and for training in righteousness, that the man of God may be complete, equipped for every good work. (2 Tim 3:16–17)

The phrase "breathed out by God" is the term for Holy Spirit that can mean spirit, breath, or wind in both Hebrew and Greek. The implication here is that scripture is both inspired by the Holy Spirit and best read through the inspiration of the Holy Spirit.

∞

Spirit of Truth,

All praise and honor, power and dominion, truth and justice are yours because you veil yourself to the ungodly and reveal yourself to seekers through your Holy Spirit.

Forgive our impatience, our untrusting attitudes, and our hardened hearts. Do not give us over to our own desires, but grant us eyes that see and ears that hear.

Thank you for the gift of your Holy Spirit, the Paraclete, who grants us spiritual gifts, unveils our hearts, and sustains us through difficult times.

In the power of your Holy Spirit, open the eyes of this new generation—grant us revival—that we might share your love through Jesus Christ.

In Jesus' precious name, Amen.

∞

Questions
1. What was Paul's letter of recommendation, and why was it interesting?
2. Why was Moses' face veiled? How does Paul use this analogy?
3. What does Paul cite in Deuteronomy 30 and why?
4. How does Paul use Old Testament scripture directly and indirectly?

Walking in the Spirit

> *Walk by the Spirit,*
> *and you will not gratify the desires of the flesh.*
> (Gal 5:16)

The Holy Spirit is not an abstract concept that merely guides interpretation of scripture. Paul sees at least two additional roles for the Holy Spirit: Spiritual companionship and provisioner of spiritual gifts.

Led by the Spirit

Thompson (2011, 61) writes: "Paul does not speak of ethics, but of how to walk, the primary term for ethical conduct." Continuing Galatians 5 cited above we read:

> But if you are led by the Spirit, you are not under the law. Now the works of the flesh are evident: sexual immorality, impurity, sensuality, idolatry, sorcery, enmity, strife, jealousy, fits of anger, rivalries, dissensions, divisions, envy, drunkenness, orgies, and things like these. I warn you, as I warned you before, that those who do such things will not inherit the kingdom of God. But the fruit of the Spirit is love, joy, peace, patience, kindness, goodness, faithfulness, gentleness, self-control; against such things there is no law. (Gal 5:18–23)

If our walk with the Lord is a metaphor for ethical living, the Holy Spirit is our walking companion, and it is the Holy Spirit that distinguishes our walking ethics from law. Notice that the fruits of the spirit appear strongly influenced by the self-described attributes of God: Mercy, grace, patience, love, and faithfulness (Exod 34:6).

Interestingly, it is this walking ethics, not the work of Christ or the strength of our faith, that Paul says distinguishes the church from law. Elsewhere, Paul writes:

> My grace is sufficient for you, for my power is made perfect in weakness. Therefore I will boast all the more gladly of my weaknesses, so that the power of Christ may rest upon me. (2 Cor 12:9)

If we stumble in our walk, in Christ we are forgiven, but it is not forgiveness in the absence of being "led by the Spirit" (Gal 5:18). Stumbling is part of the walk—we all stumble.

Everywhere in the ancient world Christian communities were in the minority where their ethical conduct set them apart from the culture around them. Paul writes:

> I appeal to you therefore, brothers, by the mercies of God, to present your bodies as a living sacrifice, holy and acceptable to God, which is your spiritual worship. Do not be conformed to this world, but be transformed by the renewal of your mind, that by testing you may discern what is the will of God, what is good and acceptable and perfect. (Rom 12:1–2)

The controlling concept throughout Paul's teaching is that the church is a holy community, set apart—"A living sacrifice, holy and acceptable to God"—in continuity with historical Israel, not by blood, but by faith (Gal 2:21–28). In this context, worship is a holy life, not music played on Sunday morning.

Spiritual Gifts

If the church is an eschatological community (a community mindful of the end-times) established by the Holy Spirit (Acts 2), Paul sees the church also sustained by the Holy Spirit through the provision of spiritual gifts. He writes:

> Now there are varieties of gifts, but the same Spirit; and there are varieties of service, but the same Lord; and there are varieties of activities, but it is the same God who empowers them all in everyone. To each is given the manifestation of the Spirit for the common good. (1 Cor 12:4–7)

Paul follows up with a lengthy list of spiritual gifts, but the list is necessarily incomplete because "to each is given the manifestation of the Spirit." These gifts are unique to each believer, but share the characteristics of being "for the common good."

Paul likens these gifts to parts of the human body,

none of which are extraneous or more valuable than another. Paul writes:

> For just as the body is one and has many members, and all the members of the body, though many, are one body, so it is with Christ. For in one Spirit we were all baptized into one body—Jews or Greeks, slaves or free—and all were made to drink of one Spirit. (1 Cor 12:12–13)

Note the reference to the Holy Spirit given in baptism. Paul's ecclesiology and ethics are thoroughly spirit driven.

∞

Holy Father,

All praise and honor, power and dominion, truth and justice are yours because you have established and sustained your eschatological community with your Holy Spirit who walks with us and grants us spiritual gifts. Be ever near.

Forgive us when we wander off the spiritual path that you lay before us and focus on other things. Be ever near.

Thank you for the many gifts of the spirit and your grace when we wander. Be ever near.

In the power of your Holy Spirit, draw us to yourself. Open our hearts. Illumine our thoughts. Strengthen our hands in your service.

In Jesus' precious name, Amen.

∞

Questions
1. What desires of the flesh most afflict you? What fruits of the spirit have you prayed for?
2. What is the Apostle Paul's metaphor for ethics?
3. What roles of the Holy Spirit does Paul focus on?
4. What metaphor does Paul employ for spiritual gifts? Why?

Selecting Church Leaders

> *There is one body and one Spirit—*
> *just as you were called to the one hope*
> *that belongs to your call—*
> *one Lord, one faith, one baptism, one God and Father of all,*
> *who is over all and through all and in all.*
> *But grace was given to each one of us*
> *according to the measure of Christ's gift.*
> *(Eph 4:4–7)*

O ne distinctive quality of the Apostle Paul is to view the church through the lens of spiritual formation whose provisioner and sustainer is the Holy Spirit. The church itself is composed of all members of God's household to whom the Holy Spirit grants gifts without discrimination.

Thus, we are not surprised to read: "There is neither Jew nor Greek, there is neither slave nor free, there is no male and female, for you are all one in Christ Jesus." (Gal 3:28) Nor are we surprised to find Paul writing a treatise on leadership to Timothy, whom he describes as "my true child in the faith" (1 Tim 1:2). In her commentary on Paul's five ministry gifts—"the apostles, the prophets, the evangelists, the shepherds and teachers" (Eph 4:11)— Carolyn Tennant (2016, 5) sees Paul's guidance to the

Ephesians addressed to the entire church, not just elders and deacons.

The Christian Family

Paul's advice to families starts with the admonishment: "Therefore be imitators of God, as beloved children." (Eph 5:1) This admonishment calls to mind— "Be holy, for I am holy" (Lev 11:44)—which Paul echoes in saying "walk as children of light" (Eph 5:8). Note the allusion to children in both passages so as to suggest that parents and other adults should be mindful of their influence in the family and their own formation.

To Greeks, this child-centric language would be shocking because the ancient family household normally tuned into the authority of the patriarchal father, the male head of household, who controlled all resources and protected family honor at the expense of other virtues. The closest relationship with the patriarchal father would be blood relatives, especially siblings, not spouses. The hierarchical relationships in the family funneled all power up to the father (Hellerman 2001, 30–41).

The egalitarian structure of the family promoted by Paul radically departed from the ancient family norm

(Hellerman 2001, 113). Relations between husband and wife (Eph 5), children and parents, slaves and owners (Eph 6) were subject to reciprocity (respecting, loving and sharing, not dominating) in Paul's framework, and this new framework then became a model for the church. However, Paul's admonishment began with a call to imitate God—Father, Son, and Holy Spirit—living in perpetual harmony.

Church Leadership

The parallel between Paul's guidance on family and church leaders is obvious and cross-referenced with the family. For elders (overseers), Paul admonishes:

> An overseer must be above reproach, the husband of one wife, sober-minded, self-controlled, respectable, hospitable, able to teach, not a drunkard, not violent but gentle, not quarrelsome, not a lover of money. He must manage his own household well, with all dignity keeping his children submissive, for if someone does not know how to manage his own household, how will he care for God's church? (1 Tim 3:2–5)

Note that Paul begins his admonition for elders with general ethical guidance, then proceeds to cross-reference the family. His guidance for deacons follows the same template, starting with ethical criteria, followed by household management fidelity (1 Tim 3:8–12).

Missing from these criteria are characteristics representative of the ancient, honor culture. An elder (or deacon) need not, for example, be a family household head, tribal leader, or civil leader, such as the elders of Israel (Exod 24). No licenses or other credentials are mentioned. If Paul (or someone else) were appointing leaders, loyalty requirements would be prominent. The guidance might look like a covenant between a lord and his vassals or, in contemporary terms, like a franchising agreement with rules about branding, consultation, training, royalties, and/or purchases from approved suppliers.

By contrast, Paul's leadership criteria flow from what we know from his letter to the church at Ephesus where he talks about Christian relationships within the household that flow from our relationship with God.

∞

Almighty Father,

All honor and praise, power and dominion, truth and justice are yours because you set aside your divine prerogatives to come down and dwell among us.

Forgive us when we get knotted up obsessing about

our own rights and privileges, fighting among ourselves rather than paying attention to the example of humility set in Christ and the Apostles, especially Paul.

Thank you for the gift of your Holy Spirit and the holy scriptures given to us that we might draw closer to you in our daily lives.

In the power of your Holy Spirit, grant us ears that hear and eyes that see that we might form a church more fitting to your example.

In Jesus' precious name, Amen.

∞

Questions
1. How did the Christian family differ from families in the surrounding culture?
2. How is the Christian family displayed in the organization of the church?
3. Why is spiritual formation interesting in Paul writing?
4. What is the structure of Paul's argument in advice on selecting elders and deacons?

Cautionary Tale

> *Our fathers were all under the cloud,*
> *and all passed through the sea,*
> *and all were baptized into Moses in the cloud*
> *and in the sea,*
> *and all ate the same spiritual food,*
> *and all drank the same spiritual drink.*
> (1 Cor 10:1–4)

*I*n the context of discussing the eating of food offered to idols, his rights as a worker in the church, and personal discipline, the Apostle Paul tells a most curious tale about the people of Israel during their time in the wilderness. During this time, they were collectively baptized in the Shekinah Cloud and the crossing of the Red Sea, and they ate spiritual food (manna) and drank spiritual water (from the rock). Yet, still they sinned and came under God's judgment (1 Cor 10:6–14).

The immediate lesson that Paul offered in this passage was about food sacrificed to idols, but the implications extend further. In spite of the advantages of good genes and a spiritual life, the people of Israel sinned and came under judgment. The obvious parallel is with the church in baptism and communion and other blessings. In the case of food offered to idols, Paul concludes: "All

164 - *Image of the Holy Spirit and the Church*

things are lawful, but not all things are helpful. All things are lawful, but not all things build up." (1 Cor 10:23)

Paul mentions law twice in this conclusion. Righteousness under law is a matter of not breaking the law—a measure of holiness—but Paul measures conduct in this statement with the words "helpful" and "build up." These are measures not of holiness (being set apart by law), but of godliness (being set apart by grace). Sacrificing food to idols is meaningless for a Christian because the idols are not real gods, but it is not helpful—others might see you and be led astray—and it does not build up the church—what are you doing in a pagan temple? Paul again concludes: "So, whether you eat or drink, or whatever you do, do all to the glory of God." (1 Cor 10:31)

Communion

This discussion of food sacrificed to idols and the caveats implicit in the tale of the people of Israel functions as a lengthy prologue to Paul's discuss of communion:

> For I received from the Lord what I also delivered to you, that the Lord Jesus on the night when he was betrayed took bread, and when he had given thanks, he broke it, and said, this is my body, which is for you. Do this in remembrance of me. In the same way also he took the cup, after supper, saying, This cup is the new covenant in

my blood. Do this, as often as you drink it, in remembrance of me. For as often as you eat this bread and drink the cup, you proclaim the Lord's death until he comes. (1 Cor 11:23–26)

The key phrase that introduces the Lord's Super is: "Do all to the glory of God." (1 Cor 10:31) Just like the Israelite people were not saved by their genealogy and spirituality, neither are Christians. In taking communion, we remember Christ Jesus and glorify God, according to Paul. Salvation is through faith in Christ by grace. Paul offers this advice once again through analogy to the experience of the people of Israel in the wilderness and a discussion of food offered to idols.

Baptism

Paul's reference to baptism cited above is fascinating. He writes: "And all were baptized into Moses in the cloud and in the sea." (1 Cor 10:2) The people of Israel were baptized both by the (*Shekineh*) cloud and the sea. This ties baptism to the Holy Spirit, much like the Apostle Peter did on the day of Pentecost:

Repent and be baptized every one of you in the name of Jesus Christ for the forgiveness of your sins, and you will receive the gift of the Holy Spirit. (Acts 2:38)

This same link between baptism and the Holy Spirit

appears elsewhere in Paul's writing:

> There is one body and one Spirit—just as you were called to the one hope that belongs to your call—one Lord, one faith, one baptism, one God and Father of all, who is over all and through all and in all. (Eph 4:4–6)

I used to think that the Holy Spirit came into our lives like a direct telephone connection to God—God's omnipresence became more real—but I gave up that idea because the first instance of prayer in Genesis was with a Gentile king, Abimelech (Gen 20), who obviously had no previous connection. Now, rather than connection, I see the Holy Spirit playing provisioning, sustaining, and formative roles in our lives.

For the early church, baptism apparently posed some problems both because of interpretation and association. Paul writes:

> Do you not know that all of us who have been baptized into Christ Jesus were baptized into his death? We were buried therefore with him by baptism into death, in order that, just as Christ was raised from the dead by the glory of the Father, we too might walk in newness of life. (Rom 6:3–4)

Here Paul sees Jesus' baptism as part of a template that we, as Christians, must follow (e.g. Phil 3:10). Elsewhere,

Paul finds some thinking that baptism implied following the baptizer:

> Is Christ divided? Was Paul crucified for you? Or were you baptized in the name of Paul? I thank God that I baptized none of you except Crispus and Gaius. (1 Cor 1:13–14)

Unity of the church required careful instruction, as in the citation from Ephesians above.

Between the quote from Peter in Acts 2 and that of Paul in Romans 6, we see the two primary interpretations of baptism: Baptism as the symbolic washing away of sin and as participating in the death and resurrection of Christ. Both are widely held views today.

∞

Blessed Lord Jesus,

All praise and honor, power and dominion, truth and justice are yours because you have given us your Holy Spirit and the scriptures for our guidance.

Forgive us when we seek to enhance our own social position in the church, find excuses to divide into factions, and lean on our own understanding.

Thank you for sound teaching, ears that hear and eyes that see. May we never wander from the faith.

In the power of your Holy Spirit, draw us together

in unity and revive the faith of our friends and family who have wandered off.

In Jesus' precious name, Amen.

∞

Questions
1. What role do genealogy and spiritual disciplines play in our faith walk?
2. What guidance does Paul offer on food sacrificed to idols? Why do we care?
3. What words does Paul use in his guidance?
4. Is God's presence exclusive to Christians? Why or why not?

Spiritual Mentoring

What are you doing here, Elijah?

(1 Kgs 19:13)

*B*arnabas mentored Paul. Barnabas' influence is obvious in Paul's effort to continue the mentoring of many churches through his letters and many individuals, including Silvanus, Sosthenes, Timothy, and likely Titus who are mentioned. Timothy is mentioned four times as a co-author of a Pauline letter; Silvanus is mentioned twice. Paul likely mentored each of these colleagues and mentioned them in letter introductions because they served as messengers to bring the letters to the churches addressed. Titus, like Timothy, is addressed in a separate letter and mentioned many times but he is more a colleague of Paul than a mentee.

Even today, co-authorship often suggests a mentoring relationship. A professor, such as my father during his time at Purdue University, might co-author papers with his graduate students and lesser-known colleagues to lend them credibility and visibility in professional circles. Oftentimes, the students wrote the papers which the professor edited. In Paul's case, his colleagues also may have served him as an *amanuensis* (or scribe), whose particular talent would be to legibly write in Greek using the least amount of parchment, which was expensive.

Mentoring in the Old Testament

Old Testament mentoring relationships resembled today's apprenticeships. Two stand out. After Samuel anointed David to be King over Israel and the Holy Spirit came upon him, King Saul unknowingly called him to play the lyre and serve as his armor-bearer (1 Sam 16:13, 18, 21). We are not told much about David's early relationship with Saul, but we know that Saul loved David (1 Sam 16:21–22), who later became his son-in-law. We can intuit from their close relationship that David learned from Saul what kings do and how they do it.

The second mentoring relationship is that between the Prophet Elijah and his replacement, Elisha (1 Kgs 19:17). Again, we are not given a lot of details about the mentoring that took place, but we know several things:

1. God asked for Elijah to call Elisha by name (1 Kgs 16:19).

2. Elisha "assisted" Elijah (1 Kgs 19:21) and traveled with him until Elijah was taken up in the fiery

chariot.

3. Elisha asked for and was granted a "double portion of" Elijah's spirit. and

4. Elisha referred to Elijah in his last moments as "father" (2 Kgs 2:12).

The context of Elisha's call is interesting because after putting all the prophets of Baal to the sword on Mount Carmel (1 Kgs 18:20), Queen Jezebel swore that she would kill Elijah, and he ran away in fear. After appearing to Elijah in a "low whisper," God instructs him to anoint Elisha as his replacement (1 Kgs 19:12–16).

What can we conclude from these two mentoring narratives? In both cases, the mentor was past his prime— and having trouble coping with it—and the mentee was called by God.

In other narratives with a mentoring theme, such as the stories of Jacob and Joseph, God himself appears to have mentored the person using affliction to help them overcome key personal flaws—Jacob his devious nature (Gen 25:27–34) and Joseph his pride (Gen 37:5–7). Once Jacob overcomes his flaw, he is given a new name: Israel (Gen 32:20). In Joseph's case, overcoming his pride (and anger with his brothers for selling him into slavery), he is reunited with his family (Gen 50:20).

Paul and Timothy

Timothy came to Paul recommended "by the brothers at Lystra and Iconium," a son with a believing Jewish mother and a Greek father (Acts 16:1–2). His personal history is recounted by Paul:

> I am reminded of your sincere faith, a faith that dwelt first in your grandmother Lois and your mother Eunice and now, I am sure, dwells in you as well. For this reason I remind you to fan into flame the gift of God, which is in you through the laying on of my hands, for God gave us a spirit not of fear but of power and love and self-control. (2 Tim 1:5–7)

Here we learn that Timothy received the Holy Spirit through the laying on of hands—a parallel to the ordination practice for elders and deacons in the church today. Lukes describes Timothy as Paul's "helper," (Acts 19:22) who Paul later calls his "fellow worker" (Rom 16:21).

Timothy frequently traveled with Paul, and Paul trusted Timothy enough to employ him as his personal emissary to the churches. From the variety of tasks to which Timothy is assigned, Timothy may have started as an assistant, but he soon graduated to being a fellow worker and possibly Paul's later replacement. Timothy may have also been imprisoned with Paul (Heb 13:23).

Other Co-authors

By contrast to Timothy, Sosthenes is mentioned only once outside of a letter introduction, where he is described as synagogue ruler (Acts 18:17). Silvanus, mentioned twice in letter introductions, was likely a fellow preacher (2 Cor 1:19), and is described as a faithful brother by the Apostle Peter (1 Pet 5:12). We can only intuit from these brief mentions that Timothy's relationship with Paul was special, being lengthier and more intimate.

The Role of Mentoring

While mentoring is part of everyone's faith journey, it is particularly important in the formation of church leaders as we see in the example of Paul's relationship with Timothy. Think of the great lengths Jesus went through to mentor the Apostle Peter as a shepherd (John 21:15–18). The young people who are personally encouraged to take a leadership role in the church as they grow up are often the ones remaining in the faith in their later years.

∞

Heavenly Father,

All praise and honor, power and dominion, truth

and justice are yours because you care for us and sent your Holy Spirit to provision, sustain, and guide us.

Forgive us for our weak hearts and clouded minds that do not harken to your advice and counsel. Be ever near.

Thank you for your patient concern for us and for our families.

In the power of your Holy Spirit, walk with us in all that we say and do.

In Jesus' precious name, Amen.

∞

Questions
1. What is special about Paul's use of co-authorship?
2. What Old Testament examples of mentoring relationships can you cite?
3. What are two characteristics of an Old Testament mentee?
4. What does mentoring look like today?

THE SPIRIT IN JOHN - REVELATION

Synopsis

While it is hard to write about other topics in the New Testament without weaving in observations from John, John's writing has at least three distinctive views of the Holy Spirit: A high view of scripture, spirit-driven accounts of pastoral care, and images of spirit-inspired worship. Only in John does Jesus say that we will be judged by scripture. John alone pictures Jesus in private, pastoral-type visits with individuals. Only John shows us multiple views of authentic worship.

The Word

And the Word became flesh and dwelt among us

(John 1:14)

*M*ore than any New Testament writer, John iden-
tified scripture as inspired by the Holy Spirit.
John's Gospel begins with this affirmation: "In the beginning was the Word, and the Word was with God, and
the Word was God." (John 1:1) In the Greek, the first three
words here parallel the creation account in the Septuagint.
If you missed the first allusion, John 1:4–5 both references
the light, an allusion to Genesis 1:3, and draws out the ethical inference in light, which John ties to a quote from Jesus:
"I am the light of the world" (John 8:12; 9:5, also Matt 5:14).

Nouns and Verbs

While the Greek in John 1:1 clearly reads word—
logos—noun, nominative, singular, masculine, Saint Jerome
(AD 382) translated *logos* as a verb—*Verbum*—suggesting
an action rather than a state of being. While the Latin,
Verbum, can have a range of inferences, including noun,
Jerome's translation suggests that John saw God's word
as synonymous with God, a stand-in for the Holy Spirit,
who is actively involved even now in God's creation. For
over a thousand years, Jerome's *Vulgate* was the primary

translation of the Bible for the church, which suggests that this interpretation of scripture was the orthodox view.

It is a small step from Jerome's interpretation of *logos* to John's *Paraclete,* whose job description is "the Helper, the Holy Spirit, whom the Father will send in my name, he will teach you all things and bring to your remembrance all that I have said to you." (John 14:26) Here the teaching available to us is the transcript of Jesus' teaching given in the New Testament.

A High View of Scripture

At the end of the Good Shepherd narrative, the Jews attempted to stone Jesus, accusing him of blasphemy. Citing Psalm 82 (also Isaiah 41:23), he responds:

> Jesus answered them, Is it not written in your Law, I said, you are gods? If he called them gods to whom the word of God came—and Scripture cannot be broken—do you say of him whom the Father consecrated and sent into the world, You are blaspheming, because I said, I am the Son of God? (John 10:34–36)

The interjection—"And Scripture cannot be broken"— is attributed to Jesus himself. While the cite in Psalm 82 disarms the Jews and is an interesting use of scripture, it does itself not mention scripture; it simply is scripture.

The interjection is uniquely Jesus expressing a high view of scripture.

This pericope stands alone and has no obvious connection to Jesus' Good Shepherd narrative and serves primarily to illustrate the push-back that Jesus received from the religious authorities. By contrast, Jesus' interjection reinforces John's high view of scripture.

This high view of scripture appears in another pericope that is often cited:

> If anyone hears my words and does not keep them, I do not judge him; for I did not come to judge the world but to save the world. The one who rejects me and does not receive my words has a judge; the word that I have spoken will judge him on the last day. For I have not spoken on my own authority, but the Father who sent me has himself given me a commandment—what to say and what to speak. (John 12:47–49)

The first part of this pericope is widely cited—"I did not come to judge the world but to save the world"—but it is taken out of context because in the next sentence Jesus says his words will offer judgment.

The next sentence is a hammer: "The one who rejects me and does not receive my words has a judge; the word that I have spoken will judge him on the last day."

Jesus says that his words—our scripture—will be the basis for future judgment of those that reject him. The final sentence serves to reinforce that point: Jesus speaks on the authority of God himself.

By citing Jesus, John is telling us that God himself has a high view of scripture. Thus, scripture is not only divinely inspired, it serves for us as law and the basis for future judgment.

Giant Angels

John's high view of scripture is reiterated in the Book of Revelations. The "take and eat" (Rev 10:9) instruction given to John by the giant angel in his vision is underscoring the importance of taking scripture seriously. References to the Book of Life (e.g. Rev 3:5) are another. When we eat something, it becomes part of us. For us, eating scripture is a poetic way to describe the process of memorizing scripture; for the Prophet Ezekiel, it describes his prophetic method (Ezk 3:1–3).

In the first century, few people could read and parchment was expensive. Memorizing scripture was an economic necessity for many people, but it served at least two other purposes.

First, scripture memorized is scripture applied in personal devotions and available in evangelism, especially in preaching. Things committed to memory are things important to us, which is obvious to those we talk to.

Second, when religious persecution is widespread, such as in North Korea today, owning scripture in any form can get one into trouble. Committing scripture to memory serves to protect the person memorizing from unnecessary harassment or, in the case of Esther Ahn Parks, to prepare herself to witness to fellow prisoners during internment (1939–1945) for her faith (Parks 2020).

Pastors in the Islamic world frequently memorize the entire New Testament much like Islamic students memorize the Koran.

∞

Almighty and Gracious Father,

All praise and honor, power and dominion, truth and justice are yours because our names are engraved on the palm of your hand (Isa 49:16) and in the book of life (Rev 3:5).

Forgive us when we fail to take our faith seriously and only go through the motions of following your teaching.

Thank you for the gift of scripture to guide us in our walk with you.

In the power of the Holy Spirit, keep our spirits and bodies strong that we might be faithful witnesses.

In Jesus' precious name, Amen.

∞

Questions
1. What evidence do we have that the Apostle John held a high view of scripture? What about Jesus?
2. What does logos mean? What difference does it make that logos is translated as a noun or a verb?
3. What did Jesus say was our judge?
4. Why memorize scripture? What is your favorite passage?

Spirit-Driven Care

I saw the Spirit descend from heaven like a dove,
and it remained on him.
I myself did not know him,
but he who sent me to baptize with water said to me,
He on whom you see the Spirit descend and remain,
this is he who baptizes with the Holy Spirit.'
(John 1:32–33)

*T*he particular form of John the Baptist's testimony about Jesus and the Holy Spirit is seldom noted. A peculiar phrase is cited twice: Descend and remain. This phrase appears peculiar because of its arbitrary and serendipitous nature. It is as though God told the Baptist to keep careful watch because the spirit could descend and remain on anyone.

This statement is particularly odd because Jesus was John's cousin—How could John not have known who the Messiah would be? After Jesus' appearance, the Gospel of John records a number of divine encounters between Jesus and individuals not recorded in the other Gospels.

Wedding at Cana

The serendipitous nature of the wedding at Cana pericope starts with the introduction: "On the third day" (John 2:1). You might ask: What happened on the first and second days? We are not told. The text comments on four previous "next days" making it impossible to tell what is meant. This suggests that perhaps the phrase—third day—is itself important, perhaps as an allusion to the creation account when lightness and darkness are separated (Gen 1:14–15).

In an off-the-cuff way, we are told that Jesus' mother attended this wedding and Jesus is also there with his disciples. Suddenly, Jesus' mother turns to him and says: "They have no wine." (John 2:3) Jesus is annoyed. "Woman, what does this have to do with me?" (John 2:4) Jesus may be annoyed, but he provides the wine.

Descend and remain. What do you do when the spirit moves?

Nicodemus

Nicodemus had every right to be confused. He began a conversation with Jesus, and Jesus immediately changes the subject. Jesus responded: "Truly, truly, I say to you, unless one is born again he cannot see the kingdom of God." (John 3:3)

The key phrase here is: Born again. The Greek literally reads "Born from above." *From above* is the preferred translation because it paraphrases and alludes to the earlier statement: Descend and remain.

In case you missed it, the Apostle John employs a Hebrew doublet in the next phrase: "Truly, truly, I say to you, unless one is born of water and the Spirit, he cannot enter the kingdom of God." (John 3:5) The phrase differs, substituting "born of water and the Spirit, he cannot enter" for "born again he cannot see." What you cannot see, you cannot enter. "Of water and spirit" likewise substitutes for "again" (from above).

Serendipity raises its head then in Jesus' summary statement:

> The wind blows where it wishes, and you hear its sound, but you do not know where it comes from or where it goes. So it is with everyone who is born of the Spirit. (John 3:8)

The following sentences, such as John 3:16, are famous but leave us with no clue when Jesus' conversation with Nicodemus ends. Verse 22 is a head scratcher—"After this Jesus and his disciples went into the Judean countryside" (John 3:22)—because Jesus met with Nicodemus at night. Did they slip out of town in the middle of the night or did Nicodemus spend the night? We are not told.

Woman at the Well

Three observations suggest that Jesus' meeting with the woman at the well is not accidental. First, Sychar is in Samaria, which most Jews avoided. Jews routinely went out of their way to walk around Samaria when traveling north to Galilee from Judea.

Second, Sychar was where Dineh, daughter of Jacob, was raped by Shechem, the son of Hamor the Hivite (Gen 34:2). Dineh's brothers, Simeon and Levi, tricked Shechem and all the men of his city into being circumcised, presumably to marry Dinah, then killed them all while they convalesced. Because of this evil act (and Reuben's sin in sleeping with one of Jacob's wives, Gen 35:22), Jacob later blessed Judah to lead the family (Gen 49:1–10). Jacob's well was later dug at Sychar.

Jesus' meeting with the woman at the well accordingly serves as a mirror image of the story of Dineh. Instead of an unrighteous man raping an innocent woman, a righteous man heals an unrighteous woman. The importance of this symbolic act is perhaps why Jesus revealed his messiahship (John 4:25–26) and the nature of true worship to the woman:

But the hour is coming, and is now here, when the true worshipers will worship the Father in spirit and truth, for the Father is seeking such people to worship him. God is spirit, and those who worship him must worship in spirit and truth. (John 4:23–24)

It is ironic that Jesus' first evangelist would be a woman of Samaria (John 4:29).

Third, King Solomon's son, Rehoboam, planned to coronated at Shechem, but because of poor judgment, he ends up provoking the Northern Kingdom to revolt. Jesus describes his mission as "I was sent only to the lost sheep of the house of Israel." (Matt 15:24) While many viewed Israel as consisting only of the old nation of Judah, the United Kingdom of Israel under King David and his son, Solomon, consisted of both the Northern (Samaria, formerly Israel) and Southern kingdoms (Judah). King Solomon's son, Rehoboam, planned to be crowned at Shechem (1 Kgs 12:1), but because of an unwise decision about taxation, the Northern Kingdom revolted under the leadership of Jeroboam.

Jeroboam worried that if the people continued traveling to Jerusalem to worship, they would return to King Rehoboam, so he cast two golden calves. He placed one in Bethel and the other in Dan (1 Kgs 12:27–29). This act was later referred to as the Sin of Jeroboam. The Samaritan religion he founded continues to exist today.

In healing the woman at the well, Jesus effectively exorcized two national curses: The rape of Dineh and the division of Israel. For us, these stories appear as a template for pastoral care under the guidance of the Holy Spirit, but for his immediate audience Jesus was uniting the lost sheep of Israel (Matt 15:24).

∞

Almighty God,

All praise and honor, power and dominion, truth and justice are yours because you guide us with your Holy Spirit and exorcize our demons.

Forgive us when we rebel like our forbearers, Adam and Eve, and reject your guidance.

Thank you for the gift of your son and our Savior, Jesus Christ, who died on the cross, was raised from the dead, and lives on in glory that we might have eternal life.

In the power of your Holy Spirit, remain close to us, even when we sin that we might be reconciled with you, our neighbors, and ourselves.

In Jesus' precious name, Amen.

∞

Questions

1. What words mark Jesus' endowment with the Holy Spirit in John's Gospel.
2. How does the Holy Spirit's presence seem serendipitous?
3. What is symbolic about Jesus' meeting the woman at the well in Shechem?
4. What is Jesus' personal mission, according to Matthew's Gospel?

Worship

God is spirit, and those who worship him
must worship in spirit and truth.
(John 4:24)

*M*ore than any other New Testament author, the Apostle John is associated with worship. John gives us numerous pictures of Jesus in the temple in Jerusalem in his I AM discourses, numerous names of God used by no one else, and numerous pictures of worship in heaven. It is significant that John relates worship primarily to the condition of our hearts—*worshiping in spirit and truth*, not to music or outer outside manifestations. This is an echo of the new covenant prophesied by Jeremiah (Jer 31:33).

Old Testament Worship

Less well known is John's extensive use of Old Testament allusions in the Book of Revelation. Often when John speaks about worship it is call out false worship. At least two Old Testament accounts appear to influence John's concept of worship: The story of Cain and Abel, and sacramental worship.

When Cain murdered Abel, it was jealousy over God's acceptance of Abel's sacrifice and rejection of his own (Gen 4:3–10). This is an account of false worship. Our worship must please God, not us. John's two lengthy accounts of worship—Jesus' discussion with the woman at the well (John 4) and John's account of the beast (Rev 13)—are narratives primarily about false worship. The account of the beast is particularly relevant today because it was about worshiping political power—the beast was a symbol of Rome.

Sacramental worship is often neglected by the modern church as passé. Listen to what Moses tells Pharaoh, the fifth time that he asks to allow the people of Israel to go into the desert to offer sacrifices (Exod 3:18. 5:3, 5:8, 5:17):

> Then Pharaoh called Moses and Aaron and said, Go, sacrifice to your God within the land. But Moses said, It would not be right to do so, for the offerings we shall sacrifice to the LORD our God are an abomination to the Egyptians. If we sacrifice offerings abominable to the Egyptians before their eyes, will they not stone us? (Exod 8:25–26)

The sacrifices in question here were not just random animals—they were animals sacred to the Egyptians. It would be like burning sport's paraphilia in front of adamant fans today.

These sacrifices were accordingly a loyalty test: "Simon, son of John, do you love me more than these [fishing]? (John 21:15) The equivalent sacrifice today would be to give up sex, power, and money—showing up on Sunday morning with your family in church is a similar sacrifice, if done with the proper attitude.

Worthiness of God

The worthiness of God, a prerequisite for worship, is a theme running throughout John's Gospel and the Book of Revelation. The controlling idea is:

> Worthy are you, our Lord and God, to receive glory and honor and power, for you created all things, and by your will they existed and were created. (Rev 4:11)

This theme runs throughout Revelation 5, but in John's Gospel, it shows up in Jesus' superabundant hospitality, an echo of Jeremiah's prophecy of the new covenant written on our hearts (Jer 31:14): The provision of wine at the wedding in Cana (John 4), the feeding of the crowds with bread and fish (John 6:4–13), and the large catch of fish at Galilee (John 21:11).

At a time when most people lived on the verge of starvation, much like the provision of manna in the desert,

God's superabundant generosity revealed his worthiness to be worshipped.

The Great I AM

The most prominent name for God is the one that he emphatically gave to Moses from the burning bush: "I AM WHO I AM." (Exod 3:14) In John's Gospel, Jesus preaches a series of laconic sermons on feast days in the Jerusalem Temple. Famous among these sermons are:

- "I am the bread of life" (John 6:35),

- "I am the light of the world" (John 9:5),

- "I am the door" (John 10:9),

- "I am the good shepherd" (John 10:11),

- "I am the resurrection and the life" (John 11:25), and

- "I am the true vine" (John 15:1).

This sermon theme even appears in Revelation: "I am the Alpha and the Omega, says the Lord God, who is and who was and who is to come, the Almighty." (Rev 1:8)

While each of these "I am" sermons tie Jesus to salvation and God, this last one seems most pertinent to the work of the Holy Spirit:

I am the vine; you are the branches. Whoever

abides in me and I in him, he it is that bears much
fruit, for apart from me you can do nothing. (John
15:5)

The continuous guidance of the Holy Spirit could not
be clearer, and it points in the direction of employing
continuous prayer throughout the day, which would give
form to a life of continuous worship.

Pictures of Heaven

The creation account starts with an important
statement of God's transcendence: "In the beginning, God
created the heavens and the earth." (Gen 1:1) Because God
created everything (heaven and earth being the spiritual
and material endpoints), he stands outside of time and
space as we know it. Eden appears as a garden, but it is
also the Holy of Holies because that is the place where
Adam and Eve commune with God.

John's picture of the city of God is a return to Eden,
although in a new form:

Then the angel showed me the river of the water
of life, bright as crystal, flowing from the throne
of God and of the Lamb through the middle of
the street of the city; also, on either side of the
river, the tree of life with its twelve kinds of fruit,
yielding its fruit each month. The leaves of the
tree were for the healing of the nations. (Rev
22:1–2)

For people used to desert life, a garden with plenty of fresh, clean water, fresh fruit always in season, and a healing tree of life are a natural image of heaven. This picture of heaven, along with the many others in Revelation, reinforces the point that God is worthy of our worship.

∞

Lord God Almighty,

All praise and honor, power and dominion, truth and justice are yours because you are the Alpha and the Omega, the one who is and who was and who is to come, the Almighty (Rev 1:8).

Forgive our uppity attitudes, blindness to truth, and deafness to the misery around us. Heal us of our attitudes.

Thank you for clean water, fruit that is ever in season, and the health benefits of modern medicine, things denied humanity in most times and places. Heal us of our attitudes.

In the power of your Holy Spirit, wake us to your majesty and worthiness of our sincere praise.

In Jesus' precious name, Amen.

∞

Questions
1. What does it mean to worship God in spirit and in truth?

2. How might sacrificial worship inform worship today?
3. What is your favorite "I am" sermon in the Gospel
   of John?
4. What is special about Jesus' "I am the vine" sermon?

CONCLUSIONS

As the Father has sent me,

even so I am sending you.

(John 20:21)

*I*f the Bible is an outreach document written by and for missionaries (Schnabel 2004, 5-6), then the Holy Spirit is the instrument of that evangelistic call. *The Image of the Holy Spirit and the Church* examines the Bible's description of the Holy Spirit from before Pentecost and the call of the church in view of current challenges.

The New Testament offers three pictures of God: The person of Jesus, Jesus' teaching about God the Father in the parables, and the founding of the church on Pentecost by the Holy Spirit. In this book, I have focused on the image of the Holy Spirit and the church.

Introduction

The introduction provides a summary of the book. It starts with a problem statement for the postmodern church that focuses on the battleground of the human heart darkened by sin, and proceeds to cite evidence from the Old Testament of the Holy Spirit's influence. The remaining sections outline the Holy Spirit's influence in the writings of Luke, Paul, and John.

The Postmodern Challenge

A survey of the challenges facing the church today shows that challenges to the church posed in the modern era lack philosophical merit. The church needs to articulate its message attending to both the heart and the mind. Church growth in the Global South is most successful when its missionaries overcome the challenge of social and economic distance. The rise of materialism in the postmodern era is a more fundamental challenge to the church because it precludes the existence of God by definition and reinforces the current crisis of authority. However, the postmodern challenge is ultimately less onerous because the church's description of the human condition rings truer than the alternatives presented.

Old Testament Images

The Old Testament introduces us to God, who takes words seriously. The story of Abram begins with a promise that resembles a coming-of-age narrative. In the Exodus, this narrative is repeated for the people of Israel, who in adversity learn to trust and rely on God. For those who refuse to acknowledge God, we see a cycle of sin, enslavement, crying out to the Lord, and God's provision of a savior. The Old Testament then walks us through a variety of divine revelations, actions, and covenants that prepare us for the better covenant in Christ and the gift of the Holy Spirit.

The Holy Spirit in Luke-Acts

The presence of the Holy Spirit is obvious in Luke's Gospel and the Book of Acts both from the number of citations and from wandering ministry, healings, and wide interpretation of law that leaves room for guidance of the Holy Spirit. The call of the church is to minister to the world adopting the footloose characteristic of the Holy Spirit that stands in opposition to the exclusivity of the temple. Meanwhile, Luke presents at least three archetypal images of the church—the formal church, the communal church, and the house church. Each must balance out the congregational role of the church with its mentoring role to individuals.

The Church in Paul's Writing

The Apostle Paul mentored the churches that he founded in their spiritual walk through his letters and visits, and he viewed them as an extension of the people of Israel. This conclusion is obvious from Paul's use of

Old Testament scripture and his view of the Holy Spirit as a spiritual mentor and grantor of spiritual gifts for ministry. Paul also promoted an egalitarian interpretation of relations within the family that he later used as a model for the church. Paul viewed the distinctiveness of the church as arising from its pursuit of holiness in an unholy cultural context. Mentoring thus played a special role in Paul's approach to developing church leaders, such as Timothy.

The Spirit in John-Revelation

While it is hard to write about other topics in the New Testament without weaving in observations from John, John's writing has at least three distinctive views of the Holy Spirit: A high view of scripture, spirit-driven accounts of pastoral care, and images of spirit-inspired worship. Only in John does Jesus say that we will be judged by scripture. John alone pictures Jesus in private pastoral-type visits with individuals. Only John shows us multiple views of authentic worship.

∞

Spirit of Truth,

All praise and honor, power and dominion, truth and justice are yours because you have made your home with us. You have guided us, provisioned us, and have endowed us with spiritual gifts.

Forgive us when we take your presence for granted, have neglected your guidance, and misused your gifts.

Thank you for the many blessings, for never leaving us alone, and reminding us of Jesus' words.

Draw us to the Father. Open our hearts, illumine our thoughts, and strengthen our hands in your service.

In Jesus' precious name, Amen.

∞

Questions
1. What pictures of God do we find in the New Testament?
2. How should the message of faith be presented most effectively?
3. Where is the church growing fastest?
4. How does the Apostle Paul structure and use his view of the family?
5. What are three distinctive features of John's discussion of the Holy Spirit?
6. What are three archetypical views of the church in the Book of Acts?

REFERENCES

Benner, David G. 1998. Care of Souls: Revisioning Christian Nurture and Counsel. Grand Rapids: Baker Books.

Bock, Darrell L. 1996. The NIV Application Commentary: Luke. Grand Rapids: Zondervan.

Bridges, Jerry. 1996. The Practice of Godliness. Colorado Springs: NavPress Publishing Company.

Bridges, William. 2003. Managing Transition: Making the Most of Change. Cambridge: Da Capo Press.

Brown-Driver-Briggs-Gesenius (BDB). 1905. Hebrew-English Lexicon, unabridged.

Brueggemann, Walter. 2016. Money and Possessions. Interpretation series. Louisville, KY: Westminster John Knox Press.

Chan, Simon. 1998. Spiritual Theology: A Systemic Study of the Christian Life. Downers Grove, IL: IVP Academic.

Clowney, Edmund P. 1995. The Church. Downers Grove: InterVarsity Press.

Covell, Raph. 1998. Pentecost of the Hills in Taiwan: The Christian Faith Among the Original Inhabitants. Pasadena: Hope Publishing House.

Edwards, Jonathan. 2009. The Religious Affections (orig pub 1746). Vancouver, BC: Eremitical Press.

Elliott, Matthew A. 2006. Faithful Feelings: Rethinking Emotion in the New Testament. Grand Rapids: Kregel Academic and Professional.

Ferguson, Sinclair B. 1996. The Holy Spirit. Downers Grove: InverVarsity Press.

Finney, Charles. 1982. The Spirit-Filled Life (Orig pub 1845–61). New Kensington: Whitaker House.

Ganssle, Gregory E. 2009. A Reasonable God: Engaging the New Face of Atheism. Waco: Baylor University Press.

Hays, Richard B. 1989. Echoes of Scripture in the Letters of Paul. New Haven: Yale University Press.

Hellerman, Joseph H. 2001. The Ancient Church as Family. Minneapolis: Fortress Press.

Hillers, Delbert R. 1964. Treaty Curses and Old Testament Prophets. Rome: Pontifical Biblical Institute.

Jenson, Robert W. 1973. Story and Promise: A Brief Theology of the Gospel About Jesus. Philadelphia: Fortress Press.

Johnson, Glenn L. 1986. Research Methodology for Economists: Philosophy and Practice. New York: McMillan.

Klinghoffer, David. 2005. Why the Jews Rejected Jesus: The Turning Point in Western History. New York: Doubleday.

Lewis, C.S. 1974. Miracles: A Preliminary Study (Orig Pub 1960). New York: HarperCollins.

Longfield, Bradley J. 2013. Presbyterians and American Culture: A History. Louisville: Westminster John Knox Press.

Mahan, Jeffrey H., Barbara B. Troxelle, and Carol J. Allen. 1993. Shared Wisdom: A Guide to Case Study Reflection in Ministry. Nashville: Abingdon Press.

Marcuse, Herbert. 1974. Eros and Civilization: A Philosophical Inquiry into Freud (Orig Pub 1955). Boston: Beacon Press.

McDonald, Suzanne. 2010. Re-Imaging Election: Divine Election as Representing God to Others & Others to God. Grand Rapids: Eerdmans.

Moots, Paul. 2014. Becoming Barnabas: The Ministry of Encouragement. Herndon: Alban Institute.

Niehaus, Jeffrey J. 2014. Biblical Theology: Volume 1: The Common Grace Covenants. Bellingham, WA: Lexham Press.

Niehaus, Jeffrey J. 2017. Biblical Theology: Volume 2: The Special Grace Covenants. Bellingham, WA: Lexham Press.

Nouwen, Henri J. M. 2010. Wounded Healer: Ministry in Contemporary Society (Orig 1972). New York: Image Doubleday.

Parks, Catherine. 2020. "Esther Ahn Kim: Steadfast in Persecution." June 14. Online: https://www.thegospelcoalition.org/article/esther-ahn-kim-steadfast-in-persecution/. Accessed: 21 October, 2023.

Pentecostal Church of God (PCG). 2020. General Bylaws 2020. International Missions Center. Bedford, Texas. Online: https://uploads-ssl.webflow.com. Accessed: 29 May 2023.

Peterson, Eugene H. 2006. Eat This Book: A Conversation in the Art of Spiritual Reading. Grand Rapids: Eerdmans.

Plantinga, Alvin. 2000. Warranted Christian Belief. New York: Oxford University Press.

Presbyterian Church in the United States of America (PC USA). 1999. The Constitution of the Presbyterian Church (U.S.A.)—Part I: Book of Confession. Louisville, KY: Office of the General Assembly.

Rogers, Jack. 2009. Jesus, The Bible, and Homosexuality: Explode the Myths, Heal the Church. Louisville: Westminster John Knox Press.

Saint John of the Cross. 2006, The Dark Night of the Soul. London: Baronius Press.

Savage, John. 1996. Listening and Caring Skills: A Guide for Groups and Leaders. Nashville: Abingdon Press.

Schlossberg, Herbert. 1990. Idols for Destruction: The Conflict of Christian Faith and American Culture. Wheaton: Crossway Books.

Schnabel, Eckhard J. 2004. Early Christian Mission: Jesus and the Twelve: Volume One. Downers Grove: InterVarsity Press.

Sproul, R.C. 2005. A Walk with God: An Exposition of Luke's Gospel. Great Britain: Christian Focus.

Tennant, Carolyn. 2016. Catch the Wind of the Spirit: How the 5 Ministry Gifts Can Transform Your Church. Springfield: Vital Resources.

Thompson, James W. 2011. Moral Formation according to Paul. Grand Rapids: Baker Academic.

Thompson, James W. 2014: The Church According to Paul: Rediscovering the Community Conformed to Christ. Grand Rapids: BakerAcademic.

Vanhoozer, Kevin J. 1998. Is There a Meaning in This Text: The Bible, The Reader, and the Morality of Literary Knowledge. Grand Rapids: Zondervan.

Wenham, Gordon J. 2012. Psalms as Torah: Reading Biblical Song Ethically. Grand Rapids: Baker Academic.

Wright, Tom. 2004. Luke for Everyone. Westminister: John Knox Press.

Yoder, John Howard. 1994. The Politics of Jesus. Grand Rapids: Eerdmans.

Zurlo, Gina A., Todd M. Johnson, and Peter F. Crossing. 2021. "World Christianity and Mission 2021: Questions about the Future." International Bulletin of Mission Research. Vol. 45(1) 15–25 . Center for the Study of Global Christianity, Gordon-Conwell Theological Seminary. South Hamilton, MA.

SCRIPTURAL INDEX

(Acts continued)

ABOUT

*A*uthor Stephen W. Hiemstra lives in Centreville, Virginia with Maryam, his wife of more than thirty-five years. They have three grown children.

Stephen worked as an economist for twenty-seven years in more than five federal agencies, where he published numerous government studies, magazine articles, and book reviews. Check WorldCat.org for a complete listing of volumes available in a library near you.

Stephen has published a six-book, Christian spirituality series. He wrote his first book, *A Christian Guide to Spirituality* in 2014. In 2016, he wrote a second book, *Life in Tension*. In 2017, he published a memoir, *Called Along the Way*. In 2019, he published *Simple Faith*. In 2020, he published *Living in Christ*. His sixth book—*Image and Illumination*—was published in 2023.

He began a new Image of God series with the publication of *Image of God in the Parables* (2023).

Two books from his Christian spirituality series are available in Spanish: *Una Guía Cristiana a la Espiritualidad* (2015) and *Vida en Tensión* (2021). He also published his first book in German: *Ein Christlicher Leitfaden zur Spiritualität* (2022).

In 2021, he published his debut novella, *Masquerade,* and rewrote it as a screenplay under the title: *Brandishing the Blue.* In 2023, he published a sequel, *The Detour,* and adapted it as a screenplay.

Stephen published his first hardcover book, *Everyday Prayers for Everyday People* (2018). He also published an ebook compilation book, *Spiritual Trilogy,* that year.

Stephen has a Masters of Divinity (MDiv, 2013) from Gordon-Conwell Theological Seminary in Charlotte, North Carolina. His doctorate (Ph.D., 1985) is in agricultural economics from Michigan State University. He studied in Puerto Rico and in Germany and speaks Spanish and German.

Correspond with Stephen at T2Pneuma@gmail.com or follow his blog at http://www.T2Pneuma.net.

If you enjoyed Image of the Holy Spirit in the Church, please post a review online.

Made in the USA
Middletown, DE
30 December 2023

46585787R00136